Informal Assessment Strategies

Asking questions, observing students,
and planning lessons that promote successful
interaction with text

BETH CRITCHLEY CHARLTON

Pembroke Publishers Limited

Copyright © 2005 **Pembroke Publishers**
538 Hood Road
Markham, Ontario, Canada L3R 3K9
www.pembrokepublishers.com

Distributed in the U.S. by Stenhouse Publishers
480 Congress Street
Portland, ME 04101
www.stenhouse.com

We acknowledge the financial support of the Government of Canada through the Book Publishing Industry Development Program (BPIDP) for our publishing activities.

We acknowledge the Government of Ontario through the Ontario Media Development Corporation's Ontario Book Initiative.

Library and Archives Canada Cataloguing in Publication

Charlton, Beth Critchley
   Informal assessment strategies : asking questions, observing
students, and planning lessons that promote successful interaction with text / Beth Critchley Charlton.

Includes index.
ISBN 1-55138-181-8

   1. Educational evaluation. 2. Educational tests and measurements.
I. Title.

LB2822.75C44 2005   371.26   C2004-907123-8

Editor: Kat Mototsune
Cover Design: John Zehethofer
Typesetting: Jay Tee Graphics Ltd.

Printed and bound in Canada
9 8 7 6 5 4 3 2 1

Contents

Introduction

I've been a teacher, a writer, a broadcaster, a workshop facilitator and a literacy consultant. But, regardless of my many professional roles, I've always looked at the world through the eyes of teacher. As I look back over all those years, it's clear that my most successful professional and personal experiences were those in which I was encouraged to ask questions, to think beyond the obvious, to challenge, and to enter into a debate. These experiences usually started with a simple question:

- Do you ever wonder if… ?
- Do you think… ?
- If that's so, then what about… ?
- Have you considered… ?
- Where do we go from… ?

As simple as they seem, these are the questions that open the doors to our thoughts. In the field of education, these are the questions that we keep coming back to in professional development sessions, in the staff room, on the playing field, during recess duty, and—all too often—at staff parties. We know there's little hope in finding one correct answer, but these questions lead us to the processes of investigating, theorizing, communicating, sharing, and reflecting. They allow us to continually improve our teaching practice—they allow us to plan lessons that are more likely to ensure a teaching–learning match. These questions also allow us to know each other and our students as people. That awareness helps us acknowledge strengths and develop respect for every person we encounter throughout the day. And, finally, it's these questions that allow us to develop the 16 habits of mind (Costa and Kallick) that make our teaching more effective:

- persisting
- thinking and communicating with clarity and precision
- managing impulsivity
- gathering data through all the senses
- listening with understanding and empathy
- creating, imagining, and innovating
- thinking flexibly
- responding with wonderment and awe
- thinking about thinking (metacognition)
- taking responsible risks
- striving for accuracy
- finding humor
- questioning and posing problems
- thinking interdependently
- applying past knowledge to new situations
- remaining open to continuous learning

This book will build on the notion of questions. Well thought-out questions are an integral component of formative classroom assessment, and, as we'll discover, they are the keystones that enable a teaching–learning match. Why? A thoughtful question, used in formative assessment, encourages us to open a door. What lies beyond that door gives us insight into what a student is able to do. And, when the answer to a question is followed up by other well thought-out questions, we have a direction for our instruction.

Informal classroom assessment is not a single event; it is an ongoing series of opportunities for a teacher to create and use well thought-out questions to gather information about a student's learning. These opportunities revolve around the teacher observing a student interact with others, participate in lessons, and complete assignments. The observations are accumulated day to day. They are not standardized, nor are they intended to be. They reflect the authenticity of classroom activities, and examining them gives teachers information about the effectiveness of their planning, their teaching, and the student's learning.

Although formative assessment is informal, it is still powerful—so powerful that, when completed with an understanding of the process, formative assessment will influence standardized assessment. When teachers "on a day to day basis… accurately assess whether kids are becoming good readers, writers and math problem solvers and if those teachers are using classroom assessment smartly, then once a year test scores will take care of themselves" (Stiggins, in Sparks).

Formative assessment can occur in all subject areas, but this book will focus on creating questions and listening to answers that allow us to examine a student's ability to process text effectively. This text may be written or unwritten; it may be spoken, illustrated, or expressed in some other medium. Regardless of the form the text takes, this book will examine how formative assessment provides a teacher with an opportunity to find out how the student approaches, enters, interacts with, and uses the text.

This book is based on the educational research and experiences of many authors, but is also a reflection of my own, and my colleagues', classroom experiences. These experiences span all grade levels and all ability levels. You'll hear the voices of teachers as they ponder questions: "How do I teach a student to be a good reader?" "How do I discover what a student is able to do?" "How do I determine directions for instruction?" "How do I involve the students in their own learning?" "How do I create lessons that encourage students to stop and think about their learning?" and "How do we know when it's time to move on?" You'll also hear the voices of students of all ages. What they know about themselves as learners, what they feel makes a good lesson, and what they want us to know about their experiences in school illustrate the amazing insight of students into the learning process.

The questions that frame any professional's life and learning are the result of life's circumstances, the research of colleagues that allows us to see how lines of thinking converge and diverge, the simple comments of those we chat with each day, and those 3 a.m. thoughts that jolt us awake and cause us to wonder what something means. Throughout my career in education, there have been pivotal moments when the research of others has caused me to reflect, rethink, and renew my focus. Discovering Marie Clay's work was one of those points; although most well-known for her development of Reading Recovery, Clay's observations about students as learners opened my eyes to the true meaning of building on success. Many other educational researchers, mentioned throughout this book, encouraged me to continue questioning. The book *Mosaic of Thought* by Ellin Keene and Susan Zimmermann, written in such a welcoming style, allowed me to place

"There are things that are known and things that are unknown; in between there are doors."
— Anonymous

"Good formative assessment processes give teachers evidence that students are progressing, and that's what will keep them going. Formative assessment gives teachers confidence that they're getting better and better. Students and teachers feel in control."
— Stiggins (in Sparks)

> "You can tell whether a man is clever by his answers. You can tell whether a man is wise by his questions."
>
> — Naguib Mahfouz
> (Nobel Prize Winner)

research about literacy in a context that was real and usuable. And like all good research, it answered some questions, but encouraged me to ask more.

My life outside the classroom has been full of opportunities to question and to learn. As a child, I listened to supper table conversations about equity, diversity, and the state of the world. These conversations, infused with humor and love, revolved around the importance of respect and the acknowledgment of the strengths of an individual. Then, when my world expanded beyond the sheltered walls of my home, and my supper table turned into the local fast-food outlet, I met Tom. From that moment to now, after of 28 years of marriage, Tom continues to be another source of inspiration. And now our children, Matt and Michèle, continue in footsteps of the family.

I'd like to thank the many educational researchers who informed my research as well as the many teachers and students of the Scarborough District School Board, the Halifax Regional School Board, Saltus Grammar School (Bermuda), Mount Saint Vincent University, and Erdiston College (Barbados). These people provided the opportunities to observe how students respond to assessments, how to question the credibility of the information gathered, and how to determine the usefulness of the information when making instructional decisions.

So, let's begin. We'll start with a question, and hopefully we'll never stop asking questions.

1

Getting to Successful Lessons

"What's the secret to really good teaching?" My initial response is to say that there's really no one secret. Or, perhaps more correctly, if there is one secret, I don't know it. But here's what I do know… so far.

I've been teaching since 1976. As I look back (and that's a long way back), I realize that along the way there were hints about the answer to what effective teaching was, but I didn't always recognize the hints for what they were.

For example, after what I felt was a particularly successful lesson, I spent some time wondering why it was successful. The obvious answer seemed to be that the lesson was well-planned, my goals were clear, the students had fun with the activity, and there was evidence of success in the students' written and oral work. So I used good planning, enjoyment of the activity, and successful completion of assignments as the criteria for defining "good" lessons, and I searched for lessons that followed a similar format. While sometimes these follow-up lessons worked well, others missed the mark completely. Despite my hours of preparation, during which I drew on everything I knew as a teacher, I created many lessons that were wonderful and perhaps just as many that could only be classified as duds. I realized that "Good intentions and expertise are necessary but not sufficient to assure successful learning" (Wayne Otto in Wilhelm, p. 5.)

Needless to say, my goal was to change that ratio or leave the profession entirely. I decided on the former. I went back to the drawing board. After lots of questions, some reflection, lots of reading, and lots of conferring with other teachers, it was clear that I needed to go beyond what I already knew, and learn more about the process of teaching and learning.

What Makes a Successful Lesson

My first realization? That, when I assumed that my teaching led to learning, I was wrong. To achieve a teaching–learning match, I had to figure out how to create lessons that formed a bridge between my teaching and a student's learning.

My second change of thought? I stopped using the words "lesson" and "activity" interchangeably. "Lesson" and "activity" are not synonyms. An activity may be the most visible part of the lesson, but it is just one small component of it. A lesson is a well thought-out plan of action that reflects an awareness of the curric-

A well thought-out lesson reflects

- the curriculum
- what the student is able to do
- what the student needs to know next
- a way for the student and the teacher to measure success

ulum, an awareness of what the student is able to do, an awareness of what the student needs to know next, and a way for the student and the teacher to measure success.

There's more. I realized that the students weren't engaged just because it was fun. Engagement is more than fun. Fun keeps kids involved for awhile, but not necessarily engaged. Real engagement is reflected in students who are involved in, aware of, and excited about making discoveries.

Finally, the indicators of success are actually much, much broader than the student's completion of an assignment. In fact, many students have an uncanny ability to "do the work" without understanding why they are doing it or how it applies to other learning situations. In the best lessons, students give indications that they "get it" during the lesson, in their conversations about the lesson, and in their follow-up assignments. To "get it" means they've learned how to do something and how it can be applied in other areas of learning—that's a real measure of success.

Here's an example of the relationship between a lesson and an activity. A student I'll refer to as Billy had difficulty working out tricky words. As he approached any unknown word, he'd become visibly tense, and begin to sound out the first letter. He'd repeat this first sound over and over again, pause, then add the other letter sounds in the word. His hope, I think, was that somehow these sounds would bring the word to him. Here's what his reading looked like:

Text: The children were walking to the mall.

Reading: *The children were walking to the m-m-m* [pause] *m-m-m* [pause] *m-m-a – l – l – l … I don't know!*

My observations of Billy's reading indicated that, in his word solving, Billy was looking at only one item of information—the individual letters of the word. To plan a lesson, I kept Billy's learning, and the following questions, in mind:

a) What does Billy know about solving tricky words? (Sounding out individual letters)
b) What does Billy need to know next? (He needs to increase his range of word-solving strategies beyond letter work.)
c) How will success be measured? (by Billy's demonstration that he has added to his awareness of word-solving strategies)

The answers (in parentheses) to these questions indicated that Billy would benefit from a lesson on how to use other pieces of information that would help him learn how to solve tricky words. I looked at what Billy was able to do (sound out the letters), and decided to build on that by teaching him a process called "chunking." I would match this word-level activity with teaching Billy a method of confirming that his word solving made sense. Here's our conversation:

Me: Billy, how are you working out that tricky word?
Billy: I'm sounding it out.
Me: Is it working?
Billy: No, I can't get it.
Me: You know how to sound out letters, but there's something else you can try. Look at the word and see if you can find a part of the word that you know.

Billy: [No response.]

Me: Look here. [I covered up the "m" and exposed the remainder of the word "all"]

Billy: That's "all"

Me: Yes. You know "m" and you know "all" Can you put them together?

Billy: M…all, m…all, mall, mall—mall? Is it "mall"?

Me: Check it—does that make sense in the sentence?

Billy: "The children were walking to the mall." To the mall! Yes!

At this point, Billy paused, looked at me, looked at the page, then looked at me again.

Billy: Oh, that's so cool! Does it work all the time?

Me: It works quite a bit. It's helpful to know how to look for parts of words you know and put them together. Then, you always check to make sure it makes sense.

Was his ability to solve the word "mall" my evidence of his success? Only partially. At this point, he had completed the activity (chunking), with a fair amount of guidance from me. I was really sure of his success when the next day, as Billy was reading, he paused at the word "carpet" and said, "I see 'car' and 'pet.' Car…pet, carpet, carpet! Hey, that makes sense. It says *The dog made a mess on the carpet.* Hey, that's funny!"

Now, here's the point of the story. I'm quite sure that Billy completed many chunking activities before (worksheets, games, etc.). But on this day, the activity of chunking was presented in a lesson that was suited to Billy. The result? Billy saw the purpose for the activity, and so the lesson was a success—there was a teaching–learning match.

And that's the key—*Billy saw the purpose for the activity.* Billy learned how to do something and, more importantly, how this information would be useful. Because the lesson matched the criteria listed above, I saw that Billy was engaged, was successful, and was enjoying his success.

As luck would have it, my rather awkward contemplations about what makes a lesson successful were aided by thinkers much greater than I. As I fumbled through descriptions of successful lessons, and students like Billy described these lessons as "cool," my niece Katie, a first-year teacher, brought the work of Mihaly Csikzsentmihalyi to my attention. Csikzsentmihalyi writes about what he calls a "flow" experience: "In flow we feel totally involved, lost in a seemingly effortless performance." He goes on in more detail: "Few things in life are as enjoyable as when we concentrate on a difficult task, using all our skills, knowing what has to be done…. It also happens surprisingly often at work—as long as the job provides clear goals, immediate feedback, and a level of challenges matching our skills." (Gardner et al.)

Mihaly Csikzsentmihalyi, meet Billy… flow is cool!

How do we get to a state of flow? Csikzsentmihalyi suggests that flow experiences occur when there's a clear set of goals that require an appropriate response, when feedback is immediate, and when a person's skills are fully involved in a task that has an optimal level of challenge that matches the person's skills (Csikzsentmihalyi, pp. 28–30).

Not surprisingly, this description of flow sounds like a definition of a successful lesson. Let's compare them:

Flow Experience	Successful lesson
• has a clear goal	• Teacher has an awareness of the curriculum standards.
• has a level of challenge that matches the skills of the student	• Teacher knows what the student is able to do.
• allows the student to fully express what is best in him/her	• Teacher scaffolds instruction on student's prior knowledge.
• is enjoyable and rewarding	• Student is able to complete the task and sees the sense of the lesson.
• provides immediate feedback	• Teacher makes and shares observations of student's work through formative assessment.

Now, when I think of a successful lesson, it is one in which the student reaches a state of flow. As an added bonus, it often leads to the teacher experiencing flow as well.

Recently, I asked many of the students with whom I've had contact to describe a really good lesson. The descriptions given by these students, aged six to 18 years old, were very clear. They said lessons should be interesting, but more than that, they said they wanted assignments to be "worth doing." They wanted to know not only what they were expected to do, but why they were expected to do it. They needed to know how to do the task. And they wanted to know if and how this task would be useful to them. Put these descriptors together and it sounds like they were looking for all the elements of flow.

Here's what a Grade 10 student said the day after her teacher taught a lesson about making predictions in narrative text:

Gina: It was so-o-o-o great! In yesterday's class, we were talking about making predictions, and last night I went to a movie with my friends and I made predictions all the way through. I kept telling everyone what I thought would happen next. After awhile, my friends told me to stop (I was probably bugging them) but it was so neat to see that predicting actually worked!

A successful lesson? I think so!

The Purpose of Formative Assessment

So, can we make connections with our own teaching or learning experiences that led to a state of flow? How do we create lessons that invoke such positive reactions? How do we create learning experiences that may allow students to experience the feeling of flow?

We'll start with a focus on taking the time to know our students as learners, and thereby discovering what they bring to the learning process. To gather this information, let's look at the power of formative classroom assessment and how it provides the foundation for successful lessons.

I've found the comments students make about teaching and education to be incredibly perceptive. They really are worth listening to.

Although this discussion holds true for all learning, my focus will be on how to process text effectively—fiction and nonfiction text of any genre. Why? Regardless of the subject taught, students need to be able to make their way through the "text" of the course. This text may be written or unwritten; it may be spoken, illustrated, or expressed in some other medium. Regardless of the form it takes, students need to learn how to process the text (of any subject) effectively.

In assessment, we listen for and observe what the student is able to do.

Listening for what a student is able to do doesn't mean that we simply applaud the student's strengths. That would be a disservice to the student, and would diminish the point of informal assessment. Once we know what the student is able to do, it's our immediate responsibility to set goals and create next-steps instruction.

Assessment, in our culture, is a word with all sorts of power. Historically, assessment was linked with being right or wrong, with passing or failing, with permission to move on or a rationale for staying put. It's also been linked with locating and defining a student's weaknesses.

But let's look at the word "assessment." The Latin root, *assidere*, means "to sit beside." I like this. It implies a casual, comfortable relationship that I feel illustrates the intentions of formative assessment nicely. As we literally or metaphorically sit beside the student, we listen and observe. What do we listen for and what do we observe? Great question—and the focus of this book. We listen for and observe what the student is able to do.

This sounds simple enough, but it's actually a major shift in our thinking about assessment. In essence, we're turning assessment on its head. Instead of using assessment to look for what's wrong (the student's weaknesses), we look for what's right (the student's strengths).

Why is this important? Let's think about the process of learning in simple terms. Learning is like putting a puzzle together. The straight base of the puzzle piece is what a student knows—it's the foundation, what the students is able to do. A teacher using informal assessment to observe what a student is able to do can identify the information included in this puzzle piece. Once identified, we ask, "What does the student need to know next?" That's illustrated by the indentation in the piece. Thinking about the best way to fill that indentation, the teacher plans a next-steps lesson. This lesson is the projection on the next puzzle piece. This projection fills the indentation and serves as the link between the known and the new. Best of all, like everything new, it opens the door to all sorts of information. Over time, and through classroom observations, the teacher continues to notice what each student knows and needs to know next. The cycle continues. Every piece of knowledge opens the door to new questions, and new possibilities for instruction.

On the other hand, if we use assessment to determine areas of weakness, our foundation is not solid; it has gaps. Our instruction may give the student a piece of the puzzle, but the piece may not connect with or build on existing knowledge. As a result, the items of information may not be able to "attach" to what is known, and the likelihood of losing the information increases. The indentations in the puzzle pieces become gaps in the foundation. Rather than participating in lessons that build on a solid foundation, the student completes activities that may amount to a series of unconnected puzzle pieces.

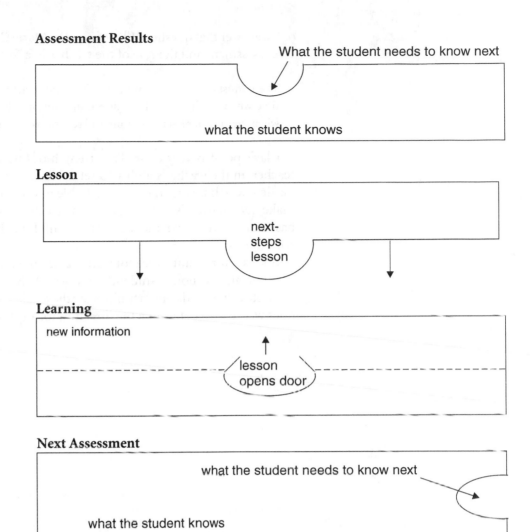

Assessment Results

What the student needs to know next

what the student knows

Lesson

next-steps lesson

Learning

new information

lesson opens door

Next Assessment

what the student needs to know next

what the student knows

Admittedly, it's impossible to be completely objective. We can't simply erase all the social filters through which we see the world. But we can try our best to listen for and record what the student does and says. Looking for evidence of what a student is actually able to do—on his or her own—may help reduce the effect of these social filters.

Let's think about Billy. If I had looked at his assessment results and determined what he couldn't do—blend individual letters to make a word—I may have spent large amounts of time teaching Billy how to do this. Billy would have built his item knowledge (the letter sounds and blending) but, without instruction on how to make sure that his blending of letters created a meaningful word, the items may not have fit into the "reading puzzle" that helps him make meaning from text.

Here's a Grade 9 student's response to a similar circumstance:

Teacher: Josh, what do you do when you come to a tricky word?
Josh: Honestly? Hmmm… I'll be honest. I just skip it.
Teacher: You skip it. Do you try anything else?
Josh: Well, I know how to sound it out. But lots of times, I sound it out and the word doesn't make sense, so what's the point of going to all of that work?

Josh is right. He could have spent lots of time sounding out a word, but unless he has some place to connect that piece of the puzzle, it's left hanging and is not much use. He needed to link his "sounding out" puzzle piece with a "meaning making" puzzle piece.

Now that I've put this premise forward, the next logical questions are

- What does the process of informal assessment look like?
- What is the teacher's role during the assessment?

13

To answer that question, I'll defer to Dr. Marie Clay, who best describes formative assessment and the role of the teacher in a formative assessment.

> There must be a time when the teacher stops teaching and becomes an observer, a time when she/he must drop all presuppositions about what this child is like, and when she/he listens very carefully and records very precisely what the child can do.

Clay's point is very clear. The strength of formative assessment lies with the teacher: in the teacher's ability to set up the assessment so that the information needed, which is what the student is able to do, is observable; then, to listen and make note of what is actually done. The teacher's role is not to interpret or judge based on previous experience with the child, or the child's siblings, parents, or community.

It's also important to see formative assessment as encompassing a wide range of observations about a student's abilities. Daily work, conversations, tests, projects, etc., all provide opportunities for the teacher to make note of what a student does well and to determine the direction for next-steps instruction.

2

Approaching Informal Assessment

Getting to know our students is our first and most important task of the school year, and it continues throughout the year. Getting to know students is the foundation of formative assessment. Each interaction we have with a student gives us a piece of information about that student as a person, as a learner, and as a participant in the classroom setting. The more we know a student, the more effective interactions are. How do we "know" a student?

Learning to Listen

The first step in knowing the student is listening to the student. Not just listening to the student's words, but listening to understand the student's words. This type of listening is called *effective listening*.

Effective listening is not easy to do, so, like all good instruction, this will begin at a level of comfort and build on shared experiences. What experience is more shared than pop culture? It's surprising how often the most casual experiences give us the greatest insight. Here are some listening quotes I've collected over the years:

> You have to listen with your eyes, not just your ears.
> — Bill Keane, *The Family Circus*

> Are you listening or are you waiting to talk?
> — John Travolta's character, Vincent Vega, in *Pulp Fiction*.

> Listening looks easy, but it's not simple. Every head is a world.
> — Cuban proverb

> We have two ears and one mouth, so we should listen twice as much as we speak.
> — Epicetus

> She was… one of those rare people who could invest as much effort in her listening as in her talking.
> — Dennis LeHane, *Mystic River*

Quotes from pop culture are a great way to encourage us to stop, to think, and—hopefully—to ask questions. These questions open the door to move from the wisdom of pop culture to the wisdom of research. My own research into effective listening began when I was at the "now I'm an adult, I know it all" age of 21. During one of our conversations, my dad pointed out that I wasn't listening to him. Needless to say, I was offended. But, even more, I was intrigued. The most accessible research on the subject was close at hand; it was research collected over many years and many varied professional experiences by my father, David Critchley.

In his work on effective schools, Dad described the power of effective listening this way:

> The supposedly necessary elements of effective schools (such as expectations, a well-defined focus, coordination, evaluation, and curriculum) although not to be diminished, were, however, all overshadowed by schools where teachers were observed to have high interpersonal skills. At the core of interpersonal skills is effective listening. (Critchley, 1992; p. 72)

These interpersonal skills are the same skills we use to get to know, to assess, and to teach our students. Effective listening is at the core of these skills. If we hope to be successful, we need to become effective listeners.

Assess Your Listening Skills

In his book, *How Many Times Must a Man Turn His Head*, David Critchley presents a simple self-assessment (see Assess Your Listening Skills on page 17) that gives readers an opportunity to think about their listening skills.

Some people feel that listening shouldn't be so much work. After all, shouldn't we be able to just relax and take it all in? Perhaps, but look at it this way. If you're speaking to someone and she or he isn't responding in the ways described in the assessment usually or even sometimes, it may be very difficult to establish and/or maintain a lasting relationship. Taking the time to listen effectively is the best way to get to know someone. And it is a sincere form of respect.

Using effective listening skills throughout the school day allows a teacher to observe the student as a person and as a learner. And during assessment, several of these questions clearly reflect the skills needed to observe what the student is able to do. See how the following examples work.

Question #5: Do you give the speaker your full attention?

Since assessment is a time to observe the student, maintain your focus on what the student is doing. As teachers, we're always looking for a "teachable moment." Teachable moments can occur all through the day, but not during an assessment. It's important to remember that our goal is to give our full attention to what the student does independently, and not to interrupt the process with a lesson. Assessment informs upcoming teachable moments right after the assessment or throughout the days ahead.

Question #7: Do you avoid jumping in and giving advice?

You're involved in an informal reading assessment. You've asked the student to read a short passage. He comes to a tricky word. You're faced with two options:

I've presented this self assessment in many professional development workshops and it always sparks a lot of discussion. Perhaps the most vehement reaction to this assessment came from a teacher who, after completing this listening survey, banged a fist on the table and said, "That's it! I could never put my finger on why things fell apart, but this survey describes exactly why I divorced my spouse!"

Without effective listening skills, we begin observing students through a filter of perception. This filter may be clouded by positive or negative classroom behavior, by positive or negative experience with a sibling or other family member, or by positive or negative experience with another teacher. Although this filter of perception is impossible to completely erase, effective listening skills enable us to see through it more clearly.

Assess Your Listening Skills

As you read each question below, take a few minutes to think about it. As you do, think about how these questions describe you as a listener, and if these questions make you want to think further about your listening skills.

Answer each question with *Usually, Occasionally*, or *Seldom*.

1. Do you try to see the world as the speaker sees it, even when the speaker's ideas and behavior conflict with your own?

2. Are you interested in the speaker as a person?

3. Do you listen willingly?

4. Can you remain calm, even though the speaker is angry or excited and may be criticizing you?

5. Do you give the speaker your full attention?

6. Do you hear the speaker out (especially at the beginning of the contact), even though the speaker is repetitious?

7. Do you avoid jumping in and giving advice?

8. When it does seem appropriate to give your observations and raise your concerns, do you raise them as questions rather than as accusations or criticisms?

9. Do you not only get the main idea, but also sense underlying feelings that may conflict with what the speaker is saying?

10. Can you keep tuned in, regardless of distractions?

11. Do you smile, nod, and otherwise encourage the speaker?

12. Do you ask questions to be sure you understand?

13. Do you refrain from pretending you understand when you don't?

14. Do you check to see if you have understood the speaker?

a) prompt the student by giving him some options for working out the tricky word

b) wait an extra second or two and observe the student's attempts

If, at the moment the struggle occurs, you "jump in and give advice," you're taking away an opportunity to observe what the student is able to do. By doing this, you're teaching, not assessing, and what you observe is not what the student is able to do by himself. By waiting an extra second or two, the student will usually show some evidence of what he does at a point of difficulty. It may or may not be correct, but the student's attempts reflect his array of problem-solving strategies. It demonstrates what he can do. This "can do" may or may not be enough to solve the difficulty, but the information gives the teacher a starting point for the next leg of instruction.

Question #12: Do you ask questions to be sure you understand?

I was listening to Cameron read. He made an error, kept reading, and then said, "Oh, wait. I was wrong." Then he went back to fix the error. Here's the conversation we had after the assessment:

Me: Cameron, at first you said this word was "pointed"; then you kept reading. When you read the next line, you decided to go back and change the word to "painted." How did you figure that out?

Cameron: When I said "pointed" I thought it was weird, but some houses are really pointed—like they have gables and stuff—so I thought, *maybe it's okay*. So I kept reading. But then, on the next line, they started talking about colors, so I thought, *something's not right*. So I went back and saw that the word was "painted" and not "pointed."

Me: Wow, that's terrific! Those words look almost the same, but you noticed that things didn't make sense, and you went back and fixed it up. Do you do that all the time?

Cameron: No, I don't know… maybe I do.

Me [taking advantage of this moment]: This shows how you are thinking about what makes sense. That's what really good readers do. Next time you read, think about what you did today.

Now that you've gone through this self assessment for listening, keep these points in your mind as you listen in your classroom, at home, and in social situations. The more you become aware of your own listening, the more you'll realize what a useful skill it is.

Through that conversation with Cameron, I got lots of information about him as a learner. Before he told me what he did, I was already pretty sure how he figured out the error. But letting him talk allowed him to clarify not just to me, but to himself, what he was able to do as a reader. He saw his problem solving lead to success.

Now, let's go back to question 7, "Do you avoid jumping in and giving advice?" Imagine if, when Cameron made the error on the word, I had simply told him the correct answer. What a lost opportunity it would have been.

Listening to Learn

Teachers who are able to listen effectively are teachers who are one giant step closer to discovering the "secret" of great teaching. In addition to knowledge of their subject, pedagogical methods, and curriculum standards, listening effectively is the primary skill that enables teachers to know their students as learners and as people. As a result, teachers who listen effectively are the ones who come closest to creating a sense of flow in a classroom.

September Notes

At the beginning of the school year, make it your goal to listen, watch, and make lots of notes about your students. To organize these notes, start with a simple September Notebook, and devote a page to each student (see September Notes on page 22). Throughout the day, carry a package of sticky notes and jot down things you notice about each student. These notes are about things said, things done, levels of comfort in each subject area, areas of interest, social interactions, etc.—anything that helps you make an image of the child as a person and as a learner. At first, there might not be any rhyme or reason to these notes, and they may not be very well organized. They will cover a range of subjects and a range of information. Don't worry; your goal, at this point, is simply to gather information.

After a few days, read over the notes on each student's page. As you read, you'll notice that there are certain trends developing. These trends will help you organize the notes in a way that reflects the student's strengths, interests, and preferred learning styles. These pieces of information help you create each student's profile. As you look at your notes, ask yourself:

- Do the notes give me information about what the student is able to do?
- Do the notes, in combination with my knowledge of the curriculum standards, give me information that will help me plan the next steps in instruction?

If you can answer these questions with, "yes," you're looking for what a student is able to do. You have the information needed to build instruction on a solid foundation and to create a successful teaching–learning match. If you find that your notes are focused on what the student has difficulty with, make it tomorrow's goal to search for evidence of what a student is able to do.

On the next two pages are examples of a page from one of my September Notebooks: the first with things I noticed jotted on sticky notes; the second with the notes organized.

"The power of teaching is often in the moment to moment interactions we have with individuals or groups…. The more skilled we can become at observing… and interacting… the higher the achievement."
(Pinnell)

September Notes Sample 1

Name of Student: *Jim*

reads accurately but haltingly

watches others while they're talking

stops at tricky words and asks for help

keen to start writing — then asked lots of questions about if he was doing it right

very attentive during read alouds

lots of ideas during the brainstorm about choosing books

seems very focused on "being correct" – hesitant to try something without asking if it's o.k.

read hockey poem fluently

interested in Greek mythology mysteries

September Notes Sample 2

Name of Student: *Jim*

Reading
– reads accurately, in one- to three-word phrases
– notices tricky words and asks for help
– asked for books about Greek mythology, hockey and mysteries
– read hockey poem fluently!

Writing
– lots of ideas during prewriting activity
– keen to start writing; asked for help when faced with a difficult spelling
– wants to make sure his written work is correct

Speaking/Listening
– attentive while classmates are speaking
– enjoys listening to stories read aloud
– keeps his eyes on the speaker

September Notes

Name of Student: _____

3

A Formative Reading Assessment

The formative reading assessment in this book is presented in the form of a "reading record." It gives information about how a student approaches the experience of reading, interacts with a text, and uses the information in the text. This reading record is based on the research of Kenneth and Yetta Goodman (Miscue Analysis), Carolyn Burke (Reader Interview), and Marie Clay (Running Record). Over the years, based on my own questions and classroom experiences with informal reading assessment, I've made a few adaptations, so you will find parts that are recognizable and parts that are new. This reading record is comprised of

The form of reading record presented here can be used at any grade level.

- a conversation with the student
- a method of determining the student's reading accuracy
- a method of determining the student's fluency
- a written code to record the student's reading
- a method to analyze the student's errors and problem-solving abilities
- a comprehension assessment
- a summing-up conversation with the student

Acquiring Information

Listening to and creating a written record of a student's reading gives a teacher quantitative and qualitative information about a student's reading.

Quantitative information includes

- the student's rate of accuracy
- the student's level of fluency
- the instructional reading level
- the student's independent reading level

Just as important is the qualitative information:

- how the student views himself or herself as a reader
- how the student views the reading process
- the sources of information a student uses to process text
- the problem-solving strategies the student has under control
- the range of comprehension strategies the student uses

A Definition of Reading

Use of Marie Clay's definition of "reading" will maintain clarity of the term:

> Reading is a meaning-making problem-solving activity that increases in power and flexibility the more it is practiced.

Reading is meaning making

Right from the beginning, it's clear that the purpose for reading goes well beyond getting the words right. Notice that this definition doesn't indicate that the meaning or the message is given to the reader. It's up to the reader to make meaning by working with the text, questioning the text, and thinking through the text.

Reading is problem solving

As we read, we know that the text we read should make sense, use an identifiable grammatical structure, and match the anticipated visual patterns of words we know. We notice when things go awry (when we make an error), and we search for ways to work it out. Then we check that our attempts at fixing the error re-establish the meaning of the passage. Searching, noticing, and checking (see page 40) are problem-solving strategies.

Reading is an activity

The only apparent activity in reading is staring at a page and occasionally calling forth the energy to turn that page. But appearances are deceiving! As we stare at a page, our brain is abuzz with activity. A formative reading assessment gives teachers a window into this activity.

Reading increases in power and flexibility the more it is practised

The more we read, the better readers we become. Students who practise by spending time with books that provide just enough challenge will become better readers. Students who practise by spending time with books that are too hard are not likely to increase the power of their reading.

Important Reminders

1. Remember the Goal of Assessment

The goal of assessment is to determine a student's strengths.

Our goal is not to come out with a statement such as, "She is in Grade 5 and is only reading at a Grade 2 level. She doesn't understand what she reads." This statement is totally disempowering—it's a statement of only what the student can't do (she can't read at grade level, she can't understand); therefore, it gives us no foundation on which to build instruction. Our goal is also not a statement like this: "He's reading at grade level." Although this may sound positive, it doesn't give us any information on which to build. What exactly did this student do well; what are the next steps for his instruction?

What is our goal? Something like this:

She is in Grade 5 and is comfortable reading books at a Grade 2 level. At this level, she sounds fluent and is able to read most of the words correctly. She can pick up some information about the passage, but needs instruction in how to connect what she knows with the new information in the text. This will be a good level for instruction in accessing and applying prior knowledge to a new text.

It may also be something as simple as this: "He is able to read grade-level fiction accurately and fluently. He is ready to apply what he knows about predicting outcomes in fiction to nonfiction text."

These statements are empowering. They give the teacher a place to start: a text level for instruction and to focus instruction. So, as we assess, we have two questions in our mind: "What is this student able to do by herself or himself?" and "What are the next steps for instruction?"

2. Remember to Observe

An assessment is a time to observe, not teach. Use your listening skills, allow an extra second or two of "wait time," and make a concerted effort not to prompt, give hints, or teach. Then, when you're finished the assessment, you know you have a picture of what the student is able to do. With your awareness of the curriculum standards and the reading process, you can begin to plan what the student needs to know next.

3. Remember to Place the Assessment in Context

This informal assessment, like any assessment, gives a picture of what the student is able to do on that day. And while trends can be extrapolated from this information, teachers should never view assessment results without question. Any assessment is just one piece of information about a student's learning—teachers should view this information in light of the many other indicators they've collected about a student's learning.

The Reading Record

The reading record, as a formative assessment, gives information about how a student approaches the experience of reading, interacts with a text, and uses the information in the text.

The Conversation

Kids are very perceptive about themselves, so it pays to listen to them. Students usually welcome the opportunity to chat with someone about themselves—especially if that person is adept at listening. A good listener questions only for clarity, doesn't judge or reinterpret the answers, and reviews what's been recorded with the student to confirm its correctness. With this information, the teacher gets a sense of whether the student approaches reading with a sense of joy, a sense of complacency, or a sense of defeat. Why is this conversation important? Because how a student feels about any task affects how that student enters and completes

Allowing "wait time" is a powerful assessment practice. Not only does it give the student an extra bit of time to collect and organize thoughts, it demonstrates to the student that the teacher has time to listen. This gives the message that the teacher values what the student says and that the answer is more important than the time in which it given.

Student Questionnaire

Student's Name: _____Date: _____Grade: ____

Record the student response in the space below each question.

1. Do you like to read?

2. How often do you read?

3. What are you interested in reading about?

    Or

    What are you interested in doing in your spare time? (for the student who claims no interest in reading)

    Would you like books or magazines about _____? (use student's interest in response to question above)

4. This line gives you a chance to rate how you feel about reading. You'll see "easy" on the left, "okay in the centre, and "hard" on the right. Put a mark where you think how you feel about reading would be.

_____

EASY   OKAY   HARD

5. What do you do when you're reading and you find it difficult?

6. How do you study for a test?

7. Do you know someone who is a good reader?

8. How do you know when someone is a good reader?

the task. Entering any task with negative feelings or high levels of tension has a deleterious effect on learning.

A formative reading assessment begins with a conversation between the teacher and the student. It has always been my favorite part of the assessment. It allows me to connect with the student. It's very informal, but I always keep in mind that my purpose is to discover how my students view themselves as readers.

The questions on the Student Questionnaire (page 26) give a teacher a surprising amount of information—students actually know a lot about themselves as readers. Although this part of the assessment may be done as an oral conversation or as a written assignment, my preference is to do it orally. The chance to have a conversation with any student is too much of an opportunity to pass up.

Use the Student Questionnaire as the basis of your conversation. The simple questions provide a lot of information about how the student sees himself or herself as a reader, and how he or she views the process and usefulness of reading. As you ask these questions, listen carefully. Try to clear your head of preconceptions and listen to what the student actually says. Make notes.

Examples of Conversations

Here are a few examples of conversations about reading I've had with students. Note how the wording of some questions changed, depending on the age of the student.

With a Grade 2 Student

Teacher: Do you like to read?
Jill: No.
Teacher: When you're not in school, how often do you read?
Jill: I hate reading.
Teacher: This line gives you a chance to rate how you feel about reading. You see "easy" on the left, "okay" in the centre, and "hard" on the right. Put a mark where you think your feelings about reading would be.
Jill: [points to "hard"] Hard. I know the words one day and then I always forget them the next.
Teacher: What do you do when you're reading and you find it difficult?
Jill: I sound it out.
Teacher: What are you interested in reading about?
Jill: Nothing.
Teacher: What are you interested in doing in your spare time?
Jill: Fishing.
Teacher: Would you like books or magazines about fishing?
Jill: YES! Are there books like that?
Teacher: How do you do in school?
Jill: All right.
Teacher: Do you know someone who is a good reader?
Jill: The teacher.
Teacher: How do you know she is a good reader?
Jill: Because her voice is smooth and she makes different voices for the characters. I love it when she reads us stories.

A colleague, Lynne Healy, told me about a Grade 2 student's rather frustrated response to reading: "Reading," he said, "is just one damn word after another!"

This student refers to "knowing the words one day and forgetting them the next." She sees reading as a process of remembering words correctly, not as a process of making meaning. For her, reading must be a daunting task—just imagine having to *remember* all the words!

With a Grade 9 Student

Teacher: Do you like to read?
Carla: Yes, I love it!
Teacher: When you're not in school, how often do you read?
Carla: As much as I can—everyday.
Teacher: This line gives you a chance to rate how you feel about reading. You see "easy" on the left, "okay" in the centre, and "hard" on the right. Put a mark where you think your feelings about reading would be.
Carla: [puts pencil close to "easy"] It's pretty easy… it depends on the book
Teacher: What do you do when you're reading and you find it difficult?
Carla: I just skip the word.
Teacher: What are you interested in reading about?
Carla: Romance, teen issues, people who get sick.
Teacher: How do you do in school?
Carla: Okay… not great.
Teacher: How do you study for a test?
Carla: I read the stuff over and over again, and I hope I remember the words.
Teacher: Do you know someone who is a good reader?
Carla: My friend Jim.
Teacher: How do you know he is a good reader?
Carla: 'Cause he just gets it when he reads—he really understands.

This student seems to have a confident attitude to reading. She reads a lot and doesn't express a concern about her reading. But, even though she "reads her notes over and over again," she says she doesn't do well in tests. Perhaps this student needs to learn other ways to search for information and to organize this information.

With a Grade 6 Student

Teacher: Do you like to read?
Pat: No, it's boring.
Teacher: When you're not in school, how often do you read?
Pat: Well, it's pretty boring, so I guess not much.
Teacher: This line gives you a chance to rate how you feel about reading. You see "easy" on the left, "okay" in the centre, and "hard" on the right. Put a mark where you think your feelings about reading would be.
Pat: [puts his pencil just beyond "okay"] I don't know, I guess it's okay.
Teacher: What do you do when the reading gets tricky?
Pat: I read it again and try to figure it out.
Teacher: What are you interested in reading about?
Pat: You're asking me the same questions. I hardly ever read. Only the newspaper, and some music magazines—but that's not reading.
Teacher: Would you like to have the newspaper and music magazines in class?

Pat: Well, maybe another newspaper. I pretty much read all of the local paper at home.

Teacher: How do you do in school?

Pat: Not bad… actually, I do fine.

Teacher: Do you know someone who is a good reader?

Pat: Well, I am really. I just don't like it.

Teacher: How do you know you are a good reader?

Pat: Well, I guess because I understand… but I'd rather not read.

This student sees himself as a someone who hates reading, but he actually reads a lot and has a good grip on the importance of making meaning. He just hasn't bought into "school" reading.

Measuring Accuracy and Fluency

The goal of this informal reading assessment is to find a text level that is appropriate for instruction in the next steps of reading, a level where the teacher's lesson allows students to build on what they know. In simple terms, we're looking for a text that has just the right level of challenge.

Accuracy

To begin the assessment, encourage the student to look over the section of text to be read aloud. According to the ability of the student, the length of the passage may change. At most, you'll need 200 words—but if the whole story is less than 200 words, use the number of words in the story.

The rate of accuracy recognized as appropriate for instruction is 90 to 94%. To determine accuracy, here's a simple equation:

$$\frac{\text{Total number of words—total number of errors}}{\text{Total number of words}} \times 100$$

$$\frac{150 \text{ words} - 6 \text{ errors}}{150 \text{ words}} = \frac{144}{150} = .96 \qquad \times 100 = 96\%$$

To many teachers, a percentage of 90% may seem high, but formal research and any action research I've been involved in supports this criterion for success. Why? A student making more than 15 errors in 150 words puts so much effort into figuring out individual words that there is little energy left to think about the meaning of the text. An accuracy rate of 90% means that the student needs to do some work with the words in the text, but not so much work that the student's efforts are concentrated wholly on word solving and not on other sources of information that may help work out the meaning of the passage. So, if the student is reading below 90% accuracy, choose another selection of text.

Self-Corrections

You'll also want to count the number of self-corrections. A self-correction is an indication that the student is monitoring her or his reading, and has the ability to

Once we know how the student sees himself as a reader, we need to find evidence of what he does as a reader.

As the student reads aloud, the teacher listens for and makes notes about the rate of accuracy, the level of fluency, and how the student interacts with the reading process.

Teachers can make a quick estimation of accuracy by scanning the page for what seems to be 100 words; if 10 errors are noticed within these 100 words, the teacher chooses another passage. Actual percentages may be calculated later.

approach tricky words or phrases in alternate ways. Self-corrections are described as a ratio and are calculated this way:

$$\frac{\text{Self Corrections}}{\text{Errors + Self corrections}} = \text{Self-Correction Ratio}$$

$$\frac{14 \text{ self-corrections}}{8 \text{ errors + 4 self corrections}} = \frac{4}{12} = \frac{1}{3} = 1:3$$

A ratio of 1:3 means that the student self corrects one error out of three. Ratios of 1:4 and lower indicate that the student is noticing errors and has the awareness of how to fix errors effectively. Ratios above 1:4 are a flag that students would benefit from instruction in how to monitor their reading.

When you've found a text the student can read with 90% or above accuracy, write the title and the percent accuracy on the Reading Record form on page 37.

Fluency

While accuracy is a criterion for success, it's not the only one. A true measure of a student's ability to process text effectively is the ability to read accurately *and* fluently. Contrary to what some researchers and assessment forms suggest, fluency is not simply a matter of how fast a student reads. It's much more important than speed. To measure fluency, we consider the speed of reading; perhaps more importantly, we listen for indications of

- meaningful phrasing
- expression
- intonation
- attention to punctuation
- a rate appropriate to the genre

When the measure of fluency includes the above indicators, a teacher knows the student has an awareness of how the structure of language works to create meaning. Fluent reading demonstrates the student's awareness of how the words in written text are presented in a predictable structure (punctuation, phrasing, intonation, and expression) that enables the reader to interact with the text to make meaning. A student reading fluently demonstrates an awareness of how

- reading is about more than knowing the words
- words work together to make meaningful phrases
- words may work together to allow for varying interpretations
- words and phrases allow us to predict what will come next and to confirm that what we've read makes sense
- punctuation allows us to adjust our reading in a meaningful way
- intonation and expression may be used to determine importance and to interpret the text

To illustrate how fluency works, think of a child learning to play the piano. At first, all effort is put into finding the notes and playing them in the right sequence. The playing may be accurate, but since the child is playing one or two notes at a time, there may not be a noticeable tune, and there's certainly no interpretation of the music. With practice, putting the notes together becomes more and more automatic. It becomes fluent. With this automaticity comes the child's ability to interpret the music. The same applies to reading. Once a student gets beyond word-by-word reading, he can begin to relate to, interpret and use the text.

In essence, the goal is for a student to read "like a storyteller" or speaking comfortably. To measure fluency, a rubric is useful. This rubric (designed by my colleague, Janet Bright) allows for a quick assessment of a student's reading fluency.

Level 4: mainly large meaningful phrases; expressive interpretation; aware of syntax

Level 3: mainly three- or four-word phrases; aware of syntax; some expressive interpretation

Level 2: mainly two-word phrases and some word-by-word reading

Level 1: mainly word-by-word

When you've found a text the student can read at fluency level 3 or 4, write the title and the fluency level on the Reading Record form on page 37.

It has been my experience that a student reading a text accurately and fluently either understands the text *or* is reading at a good level for instruction in how to comprehend the text. The "*or*" is an important distinction. We know that many students sound like good readers, but may have difficulty understanding what they read. One student who read like he was ready to give Lord Laurence Olivier a run for his money said, "Yeah, I sound great, but I don't understand a thing I read. Teachers are always asking me to read, 'cause I sound so good. But I just don't get anything I read."

Reading Levels

Independent reading level: >95% accuracy
Instructional level: 90–94% accuracy

Once you learn how to determine levels of accuracy and fluency to measure success, you can identify a student's independent reading level (a text the student reads with above 95% accuracy) or instructional level (a text the student reads with 90–94 % accuracy). This information allows you to plan the various components of your language-arts program more effectively. The independent reading level is helpful for times when a student has an opportunity to relax and read a book that allows the reader to focus on the meaning and not be hindered by excessive word work. Instructional level is the optimum for creating lessons that ensure a teaching–learning match. Please don't settle for less. All readers, particularly struggling readers, can improve their reading when the text chosen for instruction matches their instructional level, and when they have an opportunity to practise their reading on text at their independent level.

All too often, students who struggle with grade-level text are given a slightly easier book, or have the length of the assignment reduced. But this slightly easier work is usually still too difficult. So the students continue to struggle, make little —if any—progress, and inevitably fall farther behind. The students' perception of themselves as readers continues to suffer double failure—they know they have "easier" work, but still can't complete it successfully. On the other hand, if we find an instructional text level, students hear themselves as successful readers. This success enables the students to see how reading works. Instruction at this level is much more likely to be successful, and I've found that progress is faster. In the words of a colleague of mine, "It's like when a car gets stuck in the mud; rather than sitting there and spinning your wheels, sometimes it's more effective to back up—your wheels can grab on to something and you can go ahead more efficiently." In finding an appropriate level for instruction we're looking for a level of success the student can "grab on to."

Here's an example. A high-school student came into my room full of negative attitude. As he slumped down in his chair, he told me that reading sucked. He was adamant that he couldn't read; he didn't care that he couldn't read, and nothing was going to make him try. After our conversation about reading, I found out that he was interested in boxing, particularly in the Nova Scotia boxer Kirk Johnson. I asked him to tell me about a recent fight of Johnson's. The more he told me, the more questions I asked. I wanted him to bring everything he knew about Johnson to the forefront of his consciousness. It was important that he see himself as the expert, because I was about to ask him to use this knowledge. As luck would have it, I had a short newspaper article about Kirk Johnson.

I showed the student the article about Kirk Johnson. He said, "So what? I can't read that." I said, "Give it a try." Here's the rest of our conversation:

Tim: Yeah, you want me to read so you can tell me that I'm stupid.
Me: No, I want to hear what you do when you read.

At this point, Tim started hesitantly to work his way through the article. At first, he was slow and very cautious. But as he realized that he was reading accurately, his pace and fluency improved, his posture changed, and he began to smile. After he read, the conversation continued:

Me: So, how was that?
Tim: Yeah, it was okay, but that's a lot easier than the stuff I have to read in Grade 10.
Me: You're right, it is easier, but you told me you couldn't read anything.
Tim: Well, I guess I can, but only stuff like this.
Me: Then why don't we start with stuff like this, and I'll show you how to get to harder stuff as well.
Tim: When?
Me: Now.

For a student like Tim, who had had years of experience being defined as, and therefore defining himself as, "not being able to read," the feeling of success is rare. So, as a teacher, I do anything in my power to reintroduce the student to success. Knowing how to determine an appropriate text level is the first step.

Recording the Student's Reading

In addition to recording a student's accuracy and fluency, an informal reading assessment allows a teacher to create an encoded copy of a student's reading. Some teachers create their own codes, and others choose to use the recording conventions developed by Marie Clay for use in the Running Record. If a photocopied version of the text is available, the codes can be written above the errors, and attempted word work can be indicated between the lines of text. If a photocopy of the text is not available, use the Reading Record form on page 37 to record errors and word work.

Begin collecting a file of newspaper articles, short stories, and magazine clippings that reflect a wide range of levels and interests. Topics such as sports, adventure, animals, real-life issues, fantasy, and mystery are consistently among the top requests from students of all ages.

A reading record uses a written code that can be easily interpreted by any teacher or parent who wishes to discuss the student's reading.

Analyzing the Reading Record

1. The codes that count as errors are
   - Substitutions: when a student substitutes one word for another
   - Insertions: when a student adds a word to the text
   - Omissions: when a student omits a work
   - Tolds: when you decide to tell a student struggling for a word what the word is
   - Appeals: when a student stops and asks for help

2. These codes are not errors:
   - A repetition of a word or phrase that is accurate is not an error.
   - If a student appeals for help, but then is able to come up with the word independently (without a prompt beyond "Try it"), the appeal is not counted as an error.
   - A self-correction is not an error.

3. Finally, if a student makes the same error several times, the error is counted each time. This allows the teacher to know whether or not a student notices the repeated error.

Now, scan your record and count the types of errors. How many substitutions? How many insertions? How many omissions? How many tolds? In a reading record, we count each error, but our focus is to look for a pattern of errors. For example, if a student regularly substitutes words for the words in text, you know that your focus of instruction will be teach the student to notice errors and to solve tricky words.

> *In addition to coding the errors and the self-corrections, I like to make note of anything the student says or does that gives me information about the student as a reader. So, if a student begins to sound out a word and comes up with a correct response, I write down this word work. Or if a student makes an interesting comment about the story or something noticed about the text, I write that down as well.*

You might be wondering why, when some of the miscues do not affect the meaning of the passage (e.g., substituting "adores" for "loves"), they are recorded as errors in the same way as something that completely changes the meaning. Think of it this way… a reading record is like taking a picture of a student's reading, so it should be a record of exactly what that student does. Although a single error may be the result of a student's simple oversight, we don't want to make any assumptions. So we record all errors and look to see if there's a pattern of similar errors. For example, is a student regularly omits words, a teacher needs to know; but if the student makes a single omission, we record it knowing that it may not be significant. This pattern gives us an idea of what a student is able to do when challenged, and where to focus the next steps of instruction.

How the Student Processes Text

Information about accuracy, fluency, and types of errors is helpful, but it's primarily quantitative; to assist our instruction, we need more qualitative information about how a student processes the text. The transition from quanti-

Not all things you record will reflect errors.

tative information to qualitative information comes next. The next section of the assessment looks closely at the student's errors because, believe it or not, each error gives us information about what a student is able to do (see chapter 4).

Errors, while obviously incorrect, are rarely just random guesses. Each error tells us about what information the student uses to get through a text. There are three sources of information used by a reader of any text:

- information from the meaning of the passage (we make sure that what we read makes sense)
- information from the structure of the passage (we make sure that what we read has a grammatical structure that maintains the meaning of the passage)
- information from the visual aspect of the text (we make sure that the words we read match the letter patterns we see and know how to use)

A reading record allows teachers to do more than simply code an error as wrong. It lets them look at each error to see what information was used and then, after viewing the trends of errors and reading behaviors, to determine what the student is able to do and what should be the next-steps for instruction.

Comprehension Assessment

The teacher now has a fair amount of qualitative and quantitative information about a student's reading. But questions remain:

- Is there evidence that the student interacts with the text before, during, and after reading?
- How do we know the student is able to determine the important parts of the text?
- Does the student have an awareness of how to question the information in the text?
- Does the student know how to use and/or apply the information in the text?

These are valid questions. A reading record gives us an instructional or independent reading level. But it's difficult to determine a student's comprehension from just listening to the student read. The final step in the formative assessment is a comprehension assessment that allows the teacher to gather evidence about how a student processes text.

There are many different forms of comprehension assessment. Currently, the most common form of comprehension assessment is a series of questions, asked after the student has read the passage. A student who answers a certain number correctly is assumed to "understand" the passage. I, along with many educators, feel that this type of comprehension assessment may not actually measure a student's comprehension; it may be measuring a child's ability to remember pieces of information, and his or her awareness of how the structure and patterns of text give clues.

Here's an example: Jane had very little exposure to French-language instruction. In Grade 10, she entered a school in which French was a compulsory course. One whole section of the Grade 10 French course was constructed around reading the novel *Le Petit Prince* and answering the accompanying questions. As Jane flipped through the pages of the first chapter of the novel, she knew she was in big trouble. She didn't understand a word. When written questions were assigned, she panicked… until she looked at the questions. Jane realized that the structure of the questions mirrored the structure of the text. All she had to do was to find the sentence in the text that had the same word order as the central part of the question and, chances were, that was the answer—or at least a partial answer. She passed her first comprehension assignment. It also worked with the second. And so, relying on the structure of the text alone, Jane managed to pass Grade 10 French. Did she learn anything? Maybe something about completing assignments, and how to search for structural patterns, but not a whole lot about understanding French. Did she get a great mark? No, but Jane's mark in the low 60s was enough to indicate, to someone looking only at the marks, that she had achieved some level of competency in French.

Jane's example illustrates how important it is that we look beyond the obvious when we gather information about a student's comprehension. Comprehension activities, in all subjects, should reflect the student's ability

- to use the information in the text to determine importance
- connect new information with what is known
- to formulate questions
- to predict
- to confirm
- to synthesize
- to create useful sensory images
- to infer

Depending on the subject, this information may be from a text, a conversation, a display, a mathematical equation, an experiment, a work of art, a piece of music, etc. See chapter 5 for more on Assessing Comprehension.

This is not to say that there aren't times when a teacher needs to check and see if the student has "the facts" in place. Content has a level of importance that can't be ignored. But, to get information about how a student goes beyond collecting items of information and begins to process and use that information, we need more information— information that teachers can gather from "thoughtful" (full of thought) questions. Thoughtful questions reflect an authenticity of working with text. They're not "after the reading" questions; they're "before, during, *and* after the reading" questions. These questions give the teacher an opportunity to gather information about how a student ponders or wonders about the text, and if this pondering or wondering leads in a direction that allows the student to process the text effectively.

The Summing-Up Conversation

The strength of any formative assessment comes from the usefulness of the information gathered. Since the assessment is completed on a text at the instructional level, the results should provide a logical lead in to next-steps instruction. There should be an "indivisibility" between formative assessment and instruction (Black and William).

To allow this indivisibility to occur, the formative assessment ends as it began—with a conversation between the teacher and the student. This final conversation is a dialogue. After perusing the information gathered and deciding on a few key points to highlight, you begin with a statement of what the student does well (as the passage is one the student can read with a minimum of 90% accuracy and a level 3 or 4 fluency, there will be good things to talk about), and an invitation for the student to comment on his or her reading. This is followed by a suggestion related to what the teacher perceives will be the next steps for instruction.

"Comprehension is… [a] complex process involving knowledge, experience, thinking and teaching. It depends heavily on knowledge—both about the world at large and the worlds of language and print. Comprehension inherently involves inferential and evaluative thinking, not just literal reproduction of the author's words." (Fielding and Pearson)

When we listen to and chat with a student about reading at his or her instructional level, the student leaves the assessment with a memory of hearing himself or herself read successfully. The impact this has on readers, particularly readers who struggle, is powerful. For some, it's the first time they've heard themselves read accurately and fluently in a long time.

Reading Record

Name: _____

Date: _____ Title: _____

Level: _____

Accuracy (90%+):   Fluency (level 3 or 4):

Notes (use only if criteria for success is not met):

Notes about successful reading (include samples of errors, sources of information used, trends of errors, evidence of problem solving):

Focus:

4

Observing and Recording How the Student Processes Text

Three Sources of Information

For more on analyzing a student's reading behaviors, Marie Clay's books are recommended.

Errors are not, in most cases, just random guesses. Even though a response may not be correct, a teacher should assume that the student put some thought into the response. So we examine each error the student has made.

For example, if a student substituted the word "adores" for the word "loves," we can make some assumptions about this error: the student was able to maintain the meaning of the sentence ("adores" and "loves" are synonyms), and was also able to maintain the grammatical structure of the sentence ("adores" and "loves" are both verbs). The student did not, however, maintain a visual similarity between the words.

To record this information on the Reading Record form (page 37), we record the Sources of Information used. Here's the procedure:

1. On the same line as each error, write the letters M S V (M= meaning, S = Structure, V = Visual).
2. Look at each error and ask yourself these 3 questions:
   a) Does this make sense? **M** (Did the student maintain the meaning of the passage, use information from the text, use background knowledge or the pictures?)
   b) Does this sound right? **S** (Did the student maintain the grammatical structure of the passage?)
   c) Does this look right? **V** (Did the student's attempt at the word use a letter pattern or graphophonic information that is similar to the word in the text?)
3. If the answer to any of these questions is yes, circle the corresponding letter.

	Text:	The fireman was rewarded for his bravery.
Student's Reading Record :	brazenly⁄bravery	M S Ⓥ

This student substituted the word "brazenly" for "bravery." Here's what we can assume about how student made the miscue: "brazenly" and "bravery" look similar. Perhaps the student looked at the beginning and the end of the word, and attempted to come up with a word that matched some of the letter patterns and the length of the word in the text. The attempt did not match the structure or the meaning of the sentence. But it shows us that the student is in tune with *some* aspects of working out tricky words. If our reading records indicate that the student does this regularly, this is part of what the student knows about solving difficult words. We also have an idea of what this student needs to know next. From this, we can provide instruction in how to use letter patterns more effectively *and* how to ensure that this word work maintains the meaning and the structure of the text.

Text:	The horse was next to the barn.	
Student's Reading Record :	$\dfrac{\text{truck}}{\text{horse}}$	Ⓜ Ⓢ V

In this sample, the student substituted the word "truck" for the word "horse." This is coded as an error. But let's look at that error through the filter of what the student is able to do. This miscue appears to make sense and, since truck and horse are both nouns, the structure of the sentence is maintained. The student didn't use enough visual, or letter-pattern, information to solve this word. Now that we know what sources of information the student was able to use, we think about what extra information would be helpful. Does this student need instruction in how to look more closely and get more information from the word? Then does the student need to check that the word work makes sense (check the picture and look for what is next to the barn)?

When a self-correction (here coded *SC*) is recorded, we go through the routine of asking questions twice. Once to find what information the student used to make the error, and another time to find what information the student used to make the self-correction.

Text:	The rabbit hopped across the farmer's field.	
Student's Reading Record :	$\dfrac{\text{hoped S C}}{\text{hopped}}$	M Ⓢ Ⓥ Ⓜ S Ⓥ

Since this passage came from a nonfiction text about rabbits, the word "hoped" is unlikely to be meaningful. But since "hoped" and "hopped" are both verbs, the structure is maintained. There is also a visual similarity between "hoped" and "hopped." In the self-correction, it appears that the student noticed the discrepancy in meaning, looked more closely at the word, and self corrected.

If a student gets credit for using visual information, I want to know if the information used is from the letters at the beginning, in the middle, or at the end of the word. After I circle the V, I put a small stroke above the circle to indicate the information the student has used.

woods ground	Ⓜ	Ⓢ	V	(student did not use visual information)
v – v – vee very	M	S	Ⓥ	(student used information from the beginning of the word)
likes liked	Ⓜ	Ⓢ	Ⓥ	(student used information from beginning and middle of word)

Evidence of Noticing, Searching, and Checking

- Noticing occurs when the automaticity of a process is interrupted.
- Searching occurs when you look for a solution.
- Checking occurs when you find proof that the solution worked.

Teachers have an opportunity to look into the student's brain (metaphorically, of course!) as the student reads. As we observe and make a written record of a student's reading, we look for evidence of how the student approaches text, notices errors, problem solves, and verifies the accuracy of the problem solving.

Effective problem solving is evident in every aspect of our everyday life. Picture this: You get in the car, shut the door, put on your seatbelt, start the engine, put the car in gear, and you're off. As you drive along, you automatically verify that everything feels, sounds, and smells right. The more experienced a driver you are, the more automatic this verification is. But then a dashboard alert light comes on. You notice that something's not right.

Once you've noticed, you also know that you have to take some sort of action. So you search for a way to fix the problem. In your search, you think about the possible reasons for the light coming on: you listen for unusual sounds, look at the fluid levels, check the manual, or call an expert. This process of looking for a solution is a problem-solving process called searching. The goal of the search is to take an action to fix the concern.

After an action is taken, you need to know that the action you took worked, so you check for proof. In this example, your proof is that the dashboard alert light is now off. So, once again, your driving can become automatic. This problem-solving process is called checking.

Take a minute to think about other common situations in life. A good mathematician takes note of the progression of his calculations; he searches for information to determine what went wrong, when it went wrong, and possibilities for a solution; then, when an attempt at correction is made, he checks that all of the pieces fit and the calculation once again makes sense. If we play an instrument, we notice when the melody goes astray; we search for a way to fix it; we play the melody again and we check that, in our replaying, we've regained the melody. And, when we read, we notice errors; we search for ways to correct the problem; and then, as we continue to read, we check to make sure that our reading makes sense.

As we listen to a student's reading, we are very attentive to the "hints" a student's comments and body language give us information about the student's ability to

- notice when reading falters (Does the student notice when the meaning, the structure, or the visual information in the passage is compromised?)

- search for information (Does the student have a range of strategies that allow the student to confirm what he or she has read as accurate, or to attempt to correct errors?)
- check for accuracy (Does the student confirm that this searching has reestablished the meaning, structure, and visual information of the passage?)

Here's a diagram to illustrate this process:

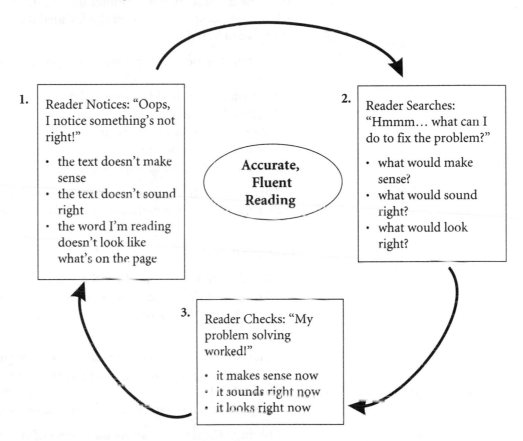

Including evidence of noticing, searching, and checking in your observations of a student's reading is helpful. These strategies are at the centre of effective processing of text, and making note of them allows the teacher to think about what's going on in the mind of the student when he or she reads, and what the student may need to know next.

Getting Evidence of Problem Solving

Observing evidence of problem solving is much simpler with younger readers. They tend to think out loud and say, "That doesn't make sense" or "I'm going to read that again" or "*Now* it makes sense!" As children grow older, problem solving becomes more internalized. The more you listen to students read, the more you'll get a feel for the subtle indicators of problem-solving strategies. If not completely internalized, noticing may be indicated by a pause or a querying look. The student may then search by rereading, reading ahead, sounding out a word, or looking at a picture or diagram. After the searching has led to a response, the checking may be a reread to confirm. Sometimes these are overt, but not always. That's why, after the assessment, it's important to have a conversation with the student about the reading. During this conversation, mention what you noticed about the student's reading, and ask the student to tell you why he or she approached the text in that way.

Example A

As a Grade 4 student was reading, the teacher noticed that she paused slightly before continuing to read. After she finished the passage, the teacher and student had this conversation:

Teacher: I noticed you paused here [points to section of text]. Why did you stop?
Student: At first, it didn't sound right.
Teacher: What did you do?
Student: I read it over in my head.
Teacher: Did that work?
Student: Yeah, it made sense then.

This conversation gives an indication of the student noticed (when she paused), searching (when she reread), and checking (making sure it made sense).

Example B

As a Grade 6 student was reading, the teacher recorded the student's substitution of "through" for "thought." She also noted that, when the word came up again, he said it correctly. After he finished the passage, the teacher and the student had this conversation:

Teacher: At first, you said "through" for "thought," but later on in the passage, you got it right. How did you figure that out?
Student: I always get those words mixed up. "Through" didn't make sense, so I figured it had to be "thought." It came up again later, so I fixed it up then.

Although there was no overt indication of the student noticing the error, his self-correction later on in the passage was evidence enough. During the conversation, he gave an indication that he was aware of (or noticed) his tendency to confuse the words "through" and "thought." There's also an indication that he involved himself in some sort of searching process to confirm or change his initial attempt.

> *Information about a student's use of noticing, searching, and checking can be applied well beyond reading text. Regardless of what students encounter, they should have an awareness of the strategies that allow them to monitor, search, and check. In math and science, a student needs to know how to notice when things don't make sense, how to search for solutions, and how to check for accuracy. When studying the visual arts or music, the processes of noticing, searching, and checking have implications for mastery as well as for appreciation of the art form or musical piece. In history, lessons are much more effective when students are taught how to notice when the sequence of events make sense, how to search for explanations, and how to check that the factors influencing historical events follow a logical progression.*

5

Assessing Comprehension

When readers process text effectively, they have an ongoing inner conversation with their background knowledge, with the words on the page, with the author, and with the concepts presented in the text. This conversation should continue after they finish reading. Let's think about what proficient readers do. Proficient readers know there is little value in collecting pieces of information from the text and trying to remember them; there are just too many pieces of information. Instead, they choose to interact with the text. This interaction is the result of a webbing of many different cognitive and affective processes. These processes, often referred to as "comprehension strategies," are in play before, during, and after any access to information. They include accessing prior knowledge, asking questions, predicting, confirming, determining importance, creating sensory images, connecting, and inferring and synthesizing. The comprehension strategies are assessable and teachable—and they should be assessed and taught—in every subject a student takes.

Where does instruction in comprehension strategies begin? As with any good teaching, instructional decisions are based on what a teacher knows about a student's learning. So they begin with a formative assessment.

The following outline for an informal comprehension assessment is based on Ellin Keene's Major Point Interview. This assessment can be used for any subject. It allows the teacher to look for evidence about how a student approaches a text, interacts with a text, and uses the information in the text. You'll notice that this is not an "after the reading" assessment; it attempts to mimic how proficient readers make meaning. Therefore, the questions about the text are asked before, during, and after the student reads. It may be completed individually or in a group. The student may read orally (if you're doing a reading record) or silently, and may answer the questions orally or in written format.

Once again, our goal is to determine *what the student is able to do*. And then, using this information in concert with the curriculum standards, making decisions about *the next steps for this student's instruction*.

A cautionary note: Basing a student's ability to comprehend on written responses is not necessarily a real indication of his or her comprehension—a request to answer in written form assumes the student has the ability to translate thought into a standardized written structure. For many students, this may not be a concern; but for some, it is. In formative assessment, it's a good idea to mix up the possibilities for responses—a variety of assessments requiring oral or written responses give the teacher a wide range of information.

An Across-the-Curriculum Comprehension Assessment

The following assessment is presented as a series of reproducible pages that include instructions and rubrics. But be aware that this is a flexible frame, with an invitation to change the wording of the questions and of the rubrics as needed.

Once this comprehension assessment is completed, you'll have evidence that the student knows what the passage is about, you'll have evidence about the comprehension strategies a student uses, and you'll know which comprehension strategies require more in-depth instruction.

This comprehension assessment is designed to measure how a student interacts with text, so a rubric is more useful than a designation of right or wrong. Rubrics give a teacher a closer indication of what a student knows and what are the next steps for instruction. I've never found a rubric, created by someone else, that provides all the information that I need. So, the rubrics are provided as guides. You and your colleagues may wish to develop your own rubrics. There are several internet sites that facilitate the creation of rubrics for formative assessment.

Before beginning this assessment, here are some simple reminders:

- This is an individual assessment, so it's a bit time consuming. Suggestions as to how to fit it into a busy class schedule are included in chapter 7.
- Don't coach the student through the task. You want evidence of what the student able to do by himself or herself.
- As the student responds, think about your listening skills. Listen to what the student says, not what you expect to hear.
- As you listen, keep the criteria of the scoring rubrics in mind and give the student credit for what he or she is able to do—unassisted. Remember, you're searching for information about what the next steps for instruction are.
- Remember that this is just one indication of a student's comprehension. It's important to base your awareness of a student's ability on a variety of formative assessments.

To complete this assessment, there is a certain amount of preparation needed:

1. Since this assessment is designed to be given at an instructional text level (90% accuracy and a level 3 or 4 fluency; see pages 29–32), teachers will need a variety of multi-leveled passages.
2. A reading record can be included in this assessment. Before beginning, select the section you wish to be read aloud. (For beginning readers, texts are short, so it may be the entire story; as readers progress, a reading record can be completed with a selection of 200 words.)

3. Teachers will need to predetermine which words to use for Question 5 (word work and vocabulary building).
4. State the directions and the questions clearly. The wording is only a suggestion. Based on the community and the shared language of that community, teachers may wish to change the wording.

This comprehension assessment is presented in two formats. The first includes all the necessary instructions, the questions, and the rubrics. At first, a teacher may wish to use this format. Once comfortable with the procedure, a teacher may want to use the short version, presented as Comprehension Assessment: Short Form on pages 55–56.

Across-the-Curriculum Comprehension Assessment

Setting the Stage for Success

Question 1 *Focus: Making predictions*

Teacher: Take a few minutes to look over this passage.

Based on what you see, what do you think this _____ (story, poem, article, chapter) will be about? Why do you think that?

[N.B. The placement of questions about making predictions may occur at any point of the text.]

Level 4	Level 3	Level 2	Level 1
Using several related pieces of evidence from the text, student makes a relevant prediction of events or topic and clearly describes how the prediction was made.	Using two pieces of evidence from the text, student makes a prediction of events or topic and describes how the prediction was made.	Using one piece of evidence from the text, student makes a prediction of events or topic and has difficulty describing how the prediction was made.	Student's does not make a prediction.

[Depending on when this question is given, the "pieces of evidence" refer to text features (such as titles, subtitles, illustrations), events in the story, knowledge of genre, or prior knowledge about the passage.]

Notes:

Teacher: Take a few minutes to read the following passage (story, poem, article, chapter, etc.) Let me know when you're finished, and we'll begin to chat about what you've read.

[This is an important step. Since the assessment may include a section of oral reading (where the teacher completes the reading record) that breaks up a student's reading, you want to be sure that the student has had an opportunity to read the complete passage.]

Across-the-Curriculum Comprehension Assessment

Entering the Text

Question 2 *Focus: Accessing prior knowledge*

Teacher: What do you already know about this _____ (topic, genre, author, time in history)?

Level 4	Level 3	Level 2	Level 1
Student gives strong evidence (three or more items of information) of using prior knowledge.	Student gives some evidence (two items of information) of using prior knowledge.	Student gives little evidence (one item of information) of using prior knowledge.	Student does not relate prior knowledge to text.

Notes:

Across-the-Curriculum Comprehension Assessment

Interacting With the Text

Question 3. *Focus: Determining importance*

Teacher: I've divided the story into _____ (two or three) parts. After you read each part, I'll ask you some questions about the _____ (chapter, story, poem, article. etc.)

Read to here. After you finish reading, I'll ask you to tell me what the key point is and some details that support that point.
[You may want to ask the student to read the first 200 words aloud—this gives you an opportunity to do a reading record.]

Teacher: Now that you are finished reading, use one sentence to describe what this section was about. What are some of the details that tell you more about your sentence?

Level 4	Level 3	Level 2	Level 1
Student gives key concept of passage and at least three relevant supporting details.	Student lists several relevant supporting details.	Student gives one relevant detail.	Student does not give a key concept or details.

Notes:

Across-the-Curriculum Comprehension Assessment

Interacting With the Text — *continued*

Question 4 Focus: *Making connections between the new and the known*

[If you have completed your reading record, you may invite the student to read the rest silently.]

Teacher: After you read the next section, I'm going to ask you to tell me what this part reminds you of.

Level 4	Level 3	Level 2	Level 1
Student describes several relevant details of an event, experience, or text that illustrate a connection to the key concepts in the text.	Student describes one or two relevant details of an event, experience, or text that illustrate a connection to some of the details of the text.	Student refers to an event or experience and makes a connection to a detail of the text.	Student does not make a connection to the text.

[Connections may be personal connections, connections to other texts, or connections to an event.]

Notes:

Across-the-Curriculum Comprehension Assessment

Interacting With the Text — *continued*

Question 5. *Focus: Word work and vocabulary building*

[Before the assessment, choose three or four words to include in this section. According to the complexity of the various segments of the passage, the positioning of this question may change.]

Teacher: Please tell me what these words mean. Now, tell me how you knew the meaning of each word.

Level 4	Level 3	Level 2	Level 1
Student defines all of the words and demonstrates strong awareness of how to search for meaning of concepts or vocabulary (e.g., prior knowledge, read on and go back to confirm, look at the root of the word and connect to the context, read ahead and go back to confirm, using text features, etc.).	Student defines most of the words and describes some awareness of how to search for meaning of concepts or words (e.g., keep reading, read again).	Student defines one of the words and describes little awareness of how to search for meaning of words or concepts (e.g., sound out the letters).	Student relies on a teacher or another adult's help to determine meaning of concepts or words.

Notes:

Across-the-Curriculum Comprehension Assessment

Interacting With the Text — *continued*

Question 6 *Focus: Inferring*

Teacher: Based on what you now know about _____ (a character, an event, an object, etc.) what can you infer about it? Tell me how you made that inference.

Level 4	Level 3	Level 2	Level 1
Student selects and combines several pieces of information from the text, clearly describes their relationship to the topic, and makes a convincing inference.	Student selects and combines one or two pieces of information from the text, describes their relationship to the topic, and makes an inference.	Student makes an inference without reference to the text information.	Student does not make an inference.

Notes:

Across-the-Curriculum Comprehension Assessment

Interacting With the Text — *continued*

Question 7 *Focus: Questioning*

Teacher: As you read this section, what you were wondering about?

Level 4	Level 3	Level 2	Level 1
Student refers to a section of text and clearly describes how that section made him/her wonder or question how the message of the text could be perceived or enhanced.	Student wonders about or questions what might happen next.	Student asks the meaning of a word or concept.	Student says he/she did not wonder or ask himself/herself questions.

Notes:

Across-the-Curriculum Comprehension Assessment

Interacting With the Text — *continued*

Question 8 *Focus: Visualizing and other sensory images*

Teacher: After you read this section, I'll ask you what image or picture you saw in your mind. I'll also ask you to describe which words allowed you to create that image.

Level 4	Level 3	Level 2	Level 1
Student refers to a group of words and describes a detailed multi-sensory image that is related to and shows interpretation of the meaning of passage.	Student describes a literal image that is related to the passage.	Student refers to a group of words and describes an image that is not related to the passage.	Student does not describe an image.

Notes:

Across-the-Curriculum Comprehension Assessment

Reflecting on the Passage

Question 9 *Focus: Synthesizing*

Teacher: Pretend someone just came in who hasn't read this. In just a few sentences, mention how the pieces of information in this _____ (story, article, page) fit together.

Level 4	Level 3	Level 2	Level 1
Using fewer than four or five sentences, student gives a very succinct, ordered overview of the passage.	Using more than four or five sentences, student gives an overview with some order.	Student gives a list of unordered events.	Student does not give a synthesis of events.

Notes:

Overview of Notes: mention strengths and possibilities for next-steps instruction

Comprehension Assessment: Short Form

Take a few minutes to look over this passage.

Question 1 *Focus: Making predictions*

Based on what you see, what do you think this _____ (story, poem, article, chapter) will be about? Why do you think that?

Notes: _____

_____

Question 2 *Focus: Accessing prior knowledge*

What do you already know about this _____ (topic, genre, author, time in history)?

Notes: _____

_____

Question 3 *Focus: Determining importance*

Read to here. After you finish reading, I'll ask you to tell me what the key point is and some details that support that point.

Notes: _____

_____

Question 4 *Focus: Making connections between the new and the known*

[If you have completed your reading record, you may invite the student to read the rest silently.]

After you read the next section, I'm going to ask you to tell me what this _____ (part, section, article, etc.) reminds you of.

Notes: _____

_____

Question 5 *Focus: Word work and vocabulary building*

Please tell me what these words mean. Now, tell me how you knew the meaning of each word.

Notes: _____

_____

Comprehension Assessment: Short Form — *continued*

Question 6 *Focus: Inferring*

Based on what you now know about _____ (a character, an event, an object, etc.) what can you infer about it? Tell me how you made that inference.

Notes: _____

_____

Question 7 *Focus: Questioning*

As you read this section, what you were wondering about?

Notes: _____

_____

Question 8 *Focus: Visualizing and other sensory images*

After you read this section, I'll ask you what image or picture you saw in your mind. I'll also ask you to describe which words allowed you to create that image.

Notes: _____

_____

Question 9 *Focus: Synthesizing*

Pretend someone just came in who hasn't read this. In just a few sentences, mention how the pieces of information in this _____ (story, article, page) fit together.

Notes: _____

_____

Overview of Notes: mention strengths and possibilities for next-steps instruction

_____

_____

_____

_____

_____

6

Daily Opportunities for Classroom Assessment

Once we know how to use informal assessment to gather information about a student's reading, we have a conceptual framework for assessing other areas of student learning. Basing our observations on what a student is able to do, we can extend the opportunities for assessing a variety of student responses in our daily classroom activities.

All too often, we assess a student's knowledge of a topic by the quality of his or her written response to a lesson: essays, reading responses, narratives, graphic organizers, etc. While these are all, at some point, valuable, evidence gleaned from written assignments demonstrates only a student's ability to "respond to a lesson in writing." We know this isn't the only evidence of a student's learning, so it needn't be the only one assessed.

With informed observation throughout the entire lesson, teachers can gather information about each student's involvement in the entire learning process. This involvement goes beyond the completed assignment and includes the student's interaction with the text or topic, and also his or her participation with classmates or group members. This information about student involvement allows teachers to notice

- how the student responds to small-group, large-group, and individual instruction
- the level of comfort the student has when asking questions
- the student's ability to listen

Think about your own everyday life. Throughout the day, you receive and give information by interpreting written text, illustrations, numerical symbols, movement, and music. You do this alone and in groups. Through an interplay of the processes of reading, speaking, and listening, you actively question, reflect, anticipate, and synthesize. You may or may not choose to write down what you've learned. You know it's not efficient to wait until the end of a learning event to put the pieces together, so you interact with the information throughout. This process is observable.

Now think about learning in the classroom. As we assess students' processes of learning, we keep in mind that throughout the lesson, we're looking for indicators of how students process verbal, written, observed, and concrete information, in individual and group settings, to build on what they know. This observation allows us to identify a student's strengths and to make decisions about directions for future instruction.

The opportunities to collect this evidence are wide-ranging and can occur at any point of the day's opportunities for learning. To collect information about a student's involvement in the process of learning, teachers draw on their own skills of communication. Effective listening is at the core.

Effective Lesson Delivery

To get an idea of how to extend assessment throughout a lesson, let's look at the steps to effective lesson delivery. The following lesson outline (based on *Reading 44: A Core Reading Framework*) allows teachers several opportunities throughout the lesson to observe student participation.

1. Tell the students the topic or strategy that will be taught and why you've decided to teach it.
2. Using a demonstration, provide explicit instruction in the strategy.
3. Ask students to participate in the demonstration and observe their responses carefully. Clarify any confusion.
4. Assign independent practice of the strategy.
5. As students work independently, observe their work and give them feedback.
6. Use these observations to inform future instructional decisions.

This lesson format allows time for students to participate in a task that is at first guided and supported by the teacher and later performed independently. In addition to teaching a specific strategy, this lesson structure allows a teacher to observe each student's level of participation during the lesson and, based on the response, to collect a wealth of information about a student's ability to respond orally, in writing, or in some other representation.

A teacher's ability to allow wait time, to respond to what the student says, to formulate questions that acknowledge what's right (rather than confront what's wrong) with a student's thinking, and to build a forward-moving dialogue is at the core of the assessment–lesson–instruction–assessment cycle.

Observing Levels of Participation

In what appear to be and feel like the most successful lessons, students respond by actively and respectfully participating in discussions, debates, and problem solving. This participation gives us a lot of information about a student's involvement in the processes of learning. It also allows us to listen carefully to what they say and how they say it. But how, in a busy class discussion, do we keep track of who is participating and what they're saying?

The teacher needs to keep track of which students are participating. I could suggest that teachers make check marks beside each student's name for each contribution, but I won't: it's contrived, it's too time-consuming, and —worse than that—students will begin to respond just to get a check mark. It's not exactly the learning environment we want to inspire. Here's what I've tried—it sounds ridiculously simple, but it works.

As I open up the lesson for discussion, I try to create a mental map of the discussion. As a student raises a hand to speak, I draw an imaginary line to that student and say his or her name in my mind. As the discussion continues, I look at and silently name each student who speaks, and I draw an imaginary line between that student and the next to speak. As the discussion continues, I'm very aware of the pattern of these lines and names. Later in the day, I recreate a map of the discussion in my head and jot down the names of the students who were involved in the discussion.

The information I get from recreating the discussion can be startling. Perhaps one of the most telling pieces of information is how often these lines end at the same students—perhaps not in the same order, but always the same students. What appears to be a lively class discussion is, in fact, a discussion between less than half of the class and me. So I have to ask myself why. We know that some people are just plain uncomfortable in this sort of forum. But we must ask ourselves why are they uncomfortable and what can be done about it.

Increasing the Comfort Level

These are all valuable questions, but it's often easier to recreate a situation than to analyze why it doesn't work. Start with what you know about students and give them an opportunity to demonstrate what they know at a level of comfort.

Consider these questions:

- Are they unsure of the expectations of open discussions? (Should this be the next lesson?)
- Are they unsure of the topic under discussion? (Have I chosen the lesson well?)
- Are they afraid of being ridiculed? (What have I noticed about the power structures among the individual students and groups of students in the classroom?)
- Do they demonstrate their learning in other ways? (I'll look for evidence of this, but I'll also find a way to invite them into the discussion.)
- Do they feel they get as much from listening as they do from speaking? (This is a possibility, but it also leads me to wonder why so many of these listening students end up asking, "So what are we supposed to do now?")

Recently, I reviewed the results of conversations with students in several Grade 7 classes. I noted their responses to the question about what they were interested in, in no particular order:

snowboarding	sports
skateboarding	biographies
hockey	autobiographies
boxing	biking
hunting	dogs
surviving in the wilderness	UFOs
the Holocaust	sign language
teenage issues	medieval times
rock bands	biology
World War II	cats
drug abuse	horses
Egyptology	how to draw
cultures of the world	biking
cars	riding all-terrain vehicles (ATVs)
wrestling	

When I tabulated the results, I found that, by a large margin, the most popular topics were skateboarding, riding all-terrain vehicles, World War II, and what students referred as "teenage issues."

Through the conversation at the beginning of the reading assessment (page 26), a teacher collects valuable information about each student's interests. Class discussions based on topics of student interest are much more likely to invite students to participate, and therefore offer an opportunity for a greater number of students to participate. Why? If students are interested in something, they probably know something about it and have an opinion about it. As a result, more students are likely to participate and we can observe what they're able to do.

Once my class had completed several lessons about effective listening and building respect in the classroom (see examples on pages 79–82), I established a time for classroom discussions. To spark the students' interest, these discussions were based on an area of conflict related to one of the topics I had identified as the most popular.

One day, we discussed a newspaper editorial about restricting the use of all-terrain vehicles to dedicated trails. I presented the editorial on the overhead projector and read it to the class. The discussion flowed easily. The comments ranged from thoughts about personal freedom to the idea of community responsibility and environmental concerns. As the students gave their opinions, I concentrated on my mental discussion map and was able to notice who participated. To my delight, students who had been hesitant to participate were offering their opinions. Then, by listening to what the students actually said and how they said it, I also collected all sorts of information about the extent to which each student was able to meet the curriculum standards for speaking and listening. These standards include

- maintaining the logical flow of the discussion
- sustaining the topic without relying on personal anecdotes
- listening effectively
- using information gathered to formulate questions
- using information gathered to confirm or reshape their opinions
- expressing thoughts clearly
- indicating that the student has considered and reflected on the opinions of classmates

Teaching the Student "How To" Acknowledge Opinion

In the midst of the discussion about the use of all-terrain vehicles, Jim and Micha offered these comments:

Jim: I just don't think it's right to drive these vehicles close to homes.
Micha: I don't care about that. It's so much fun—it's awesome to ride.
Jim: It's not right.
Micha: Maybe you don't think so, but I do—and I'm gonna keep doing it.

Sal and Mary contributed these thoughts:

Sal: If there are trails, there's less damage to the environment. Only small areas of wildlife will be hurt and not as many people will hear the noise.
Mary: I can see that, but the whole thrill of off-roading is exploring untouched areas. This can't happen if you're just driving on a trail. We need an opportunity to get out and explore new areas.
Sal: I know, but think about what this thrill means. Is it worth it to hurt the environment? Can't you get the thrill of exploring new areas by walking in the woods?

As students speak, keep these general questions in mind:

- Do the student's comments refer to the topic under consideration?
- Does the student maintain the flow of the conversation?
- Does the student allow others to speak and refrain from interrupting?
- Does the student express her or his thoughts clearly?
- Do the student's comments reflect that he or she has considered and reflected on the opinions of classmates?

Mary: Well, yeah… but it's the speed, and the bumps, and smashing through puddles.

Sal: So is it the speed or is it the exploring that's the thrill? Couldn't you do both, but in different ways?

As I listened, I was thinking about the opinions of the students. But more than that, I was observing how the opinions were expressed. Jim and Sal were defending the environmental side and Micha and Mary were defending the rights of the riders—but there was significant difference in how they expressed their argument.

Based on this observation, my next lesson focused on acknowledging our opinion and extending our thoughts by asking ourselves the question, "Why do I think this?" As I expected, Jim and Micha's first response to this lesson was, "I don't know why I think this, I just do." This is where teaching the student "how to" comes in.

Students need to know that an opinion isn't a random thought. Opinions come from somewhere—personal experiences, knowledge about the topic, and the opinions of others—and students need to tap into the origins of an opinion and think it through. To facilitate this, the following discussion frame works well:

Me: Jim, you agreed with the students who felt these vehicles should stay on trails.

Jim: Yeah, I just don't think it's right to drive these vehicles close to homes.

Me: Why do you think that?

Jim: I don't know, I just do…

Me: Think about what you've said: You don't think it's right. What makes it wrong?

Jim: I don't know… the noise… it's wrong.

Me: Carry that thought further—what about the noise?

Jim: It just keeps up, you can always hear them— speeding up, slowing down, changing gears. I don't need to hear that.

I could sense that Jim was at the end of his willingness to continue but, knowing that he had started to extend his thoughts, I asked if another member of the class would like to comment on the noise. Someone did, and then Jim came back into the conversation.

Jim: That's right. And another thing—people choose to live in the country to get away from the noises of the city. These things make a noise that's worse than city noise, so what's the point of living in the country?

After this short discussion, I could see how asking the question, "Why do I think that?" allowed Jim to get his thoughts in order and extend his opinion. I would share this information with Jim. Granted, he needed a fair amount of direction from me, but my direction in the next lesson would be decreased and my expectations would be increased. I would also be sure to give Jim wait time to think about and organize his thoughts.

If Jim had needed extra help, I planned to use a graphic organizer that allowed him to web his thoughts. Sometimes, "seeing" your thoughts helps you to consolidate and direct them.

During a class discussion, it's important for the teacher to model effective listening. Allow the student time to formulate his or her thoughts while speaking. If the student gets stumped, teach him or her to think through the idea and put it into words.

Using the Literacy Response Assessment

How do I keep a record of this sort of lesson? As I do everything—very simply. I keep an active student Literacy Response Assessment Journal (see page 63). One page, dedicated to each student, is divided into three sections: Reading, Writing, and Speaking/Listening. As evidence comes up, I jot it down and date it (so I can refer to my plan book for a detailed explanation of the lesson). The lesson described here would be recorded in the Speaking/Listening section.

To maintain a sense of the curriculum standards, I staple a concise numbered listing of the standards at the beginning of the journal. When appropriate, I make note of the corresponding expectation beside the comment about student performance.

Do I do this every day for every student? Absolutely not! For the first few class discussions, I simply guide the discussion and make general observations about the conversation. As I get to know my students, the more I know which students to observe each day, for what reason and when. I read over these notes regularly and look for evidence of learning for individual students—it's wonderful to record that a student known to be silent during discussions, begins to participate—and I look for trends among the students. This is the information that gives me suggestions for future lessons. All this information, and no written work to correct—it's a nice change in routine and it allows me to see a more complete view of each student as a learner.

The comments in the Literacy Response Assessment Journal reflect authentic classroom experiences and the student's responses to lessons. Collecting these comments throughout the term significantly reduces the effort put into an anecdotal report card—the notes are already available!

Assessing Interaction in a Small-Group Setting

At all grade levels, students are often involved in assignments that necessitate group work.

These opportunities give students a chance to collaborate, which often has a positive effect on student learning. When the purpose and goals of the group work are understood and group members' responsibilities are clearly defined, students see the group as a team and learn to develop their ability to value and share the work load. Perhaps most importantly, group work provides students an opportunity to be involved in a situation that simulates the real-life experiences they will encounter.

An ongoing assessment of all phases of group work allows the teacher and students to monitor their own level of cooperation and productivity, and to determine how this influences the outcome of the group work.

Literacy Response Assessment Journal

Reading

(this section provides an alternative to the Short Form Reading Assessment on page XX)

Writing

(this section is used to record information about the quality of the student's written responses)

Speaking / Listening

(this section is used to record information about the quality of the student's participation in large- and small-group discussions)

Teaching the Student "How To" Work in Groups

Just because group work is assigned, there's no guarantee that students know how to work in a group. Before expecting students to venture into uncharted territory, teachers need to provide instruction in how to work in groups.

Effective group work relies on many skills, and at the centre of these skills is effective listening and sharing responsibility. This chart overviews the individual responsibilities that promote successful group work:

Effective Listening	Sharing Responsibility
• listening to others without interrupting • valuing opinions of the team • asking for clarification, not judging • encouraging team members to offer suggestions	• knowing what is expected of me • staying on task • maintaining schedules for completing the work • cleaning up the work space

Establishing Teams

Groups may be assigned by

- similar interest in the topic
- mixed levels of ability in reading, writing, or technology
- mixed abilities in styles of presentation (written, oral, visual arts, performance arts, etc.)

To encourage group work, it's a good idea to start with activities that develop a sense of team among the members of a group. There are lots of team-building activities that take only a few minutes, for example:

- working together to create a series of tangrams
- creating a group picture: one person starts at the top, each team member adds the section below
- writing a group story: each member of a seven-member team is responsible for creating one element of a short story (where, who, what, how, what, how, resolution); team members work together to put these elements together to create a story. The results are usually hilarious.

Starting with an activity like the ones described allows the teacher to circulate among the groups, listen to the conversations, observe the levels of interaction, and make some preliminary observations about what's working well in the group and what may need some adjusting. It helps to get these things out of the way before the actual group project work begins.

Assessment

From the outset, it's important that students and teacher be involved in the assessment of the project. At first, the length and scope of the group project should be small—no need to start out with a group project that will take weeks; there are too many potential pitfalls. Rubrics for the students' interaction in the group can be developed by the students. These rubrics include general criteria, including

- levels of participation in group meetings
- ability to listen to the contributions of others
- sharing of work load
- responsiveness to suggestions from other members of the group

Rubrics are a useful assessment tool, but not the only one. Regardless of the rubric used, the extra comments, filled in by a teacher who is a skilled listener and observer, add significantly to the value of any rubric.

Students' rubrics should be revisited after the first short group project.

A separate rubric, rating the quality of the entire project and the contributions of the various group members, can be created by the students and the teacher.

Noticing a student's participation in a lesson and interaction with classmates gives a teacher one more avenue of insight into how the student processes the information of the classroom. As we acknowledge that not every student responds in the same way, the goal of our observations is to determine first if the student has choices, and secondly if he or she is comfortable with the choices.

To place this idea within the walls of a real classroom, consider the student who shows significant strength in written responses but is very hesitant to become involved in discussions. As teachers, we acknowledge this student's strength in written responses, but we also question whether it is enough. Doesn't this child also deserve an opportunity to develop his or her ability to respond and communicate in other ways? On the other hand, consider the student who is more than willing to participate in discussions, but does little in the area of written responding. Once again, is it enough to acknowledge this student's strengths without creating opportunities for him or her to learn how to respond and communicate in other ways? It comes down to first determining what the student does well, and then deciding on the next steps for instruction.

Being aware of a student's levels of participation, interaction with peers, and response to lessons in a variety of ways gives teachers a broader sense of the student, his or her areas of comfort, and the next level of challenge. In other words, it creates one more opportunity to establish a sense of flow in the classroom.

7

Independent Reading as a Time for Assessment

My feeling is that, regardless of grade or subject taught, independent reading time should occur. Students need an opportunity to read books of choice, and books related to the subject being taught. Time spent alone with a text at a level of difficulty that matches a student's abilities, is time well spent. This time allows a student to think about the text, ponder and wonder about its meaning, and put to use the information learned.

Since the form of assessment suggested in this book is, for the most part, is an individual assessment, teachers have every right to wonder how they'll ever get the time to assess each student—several times a year! Teachers are right to be concerned: the time needed to prepare, teach, and reflect on teaching is increasing each year. And this time is increasingly cut into by the multitude of other responsibilities faced by teachers. For formative assessment to be a regular, useful part of a classroom routine, and not just one more thing to do, teachers need a sensible organizational model. Otherwise, they may feel overwhelmed and stressed to the point where achieving a state of "flow" is not on their mind—survival is! To avoid that stress, this section will discuss an organizational model that allows teachers to gather information about their students as learners. This model allows time for an informal reading assessment, student conferencing, making decisions about instructional choices, and—last, but certainly not least—meeting the curriculum standards.

For many elementary, and some middle- and high-school classrooms, the basics of this model already exist in the time scheduled as independent reading time.

At present in many classrooms, independent reading time tends to be "free reading time." The students spend this time reading and the teacher "models" what good readers do—the teacher reads. The rationale behind the teacher reading is valid. By reading, the message the teacher feels he or she is sending to the students is that reading is something that the teacher values, it's not just something a teacher tells students to do. In some schools, the school schedule includes a time set aside each day or each week for independent reading. Everyone—teachers, students, support staff, and visiting volunteers—spend a certain amount of time reading. The goal of this time is to instill in the students a sense of the importance of reading.

Although this model may work well for proficient readers—they welcome the opportunity to have some time dedicated to "just reading"—students who struggle often don't benefit as much. Since book choice is left up to the individual, these students tend to choose books that are too difficult, because that's what their friends are reading. Even worse, they become passive and learn how to exhibit "reading behaviors" (they sit quietly, stare at the page, and occasionally turn the page). Many times, boredom sets in and misbehavior results.

Although teachers may be aware that the student is choosing a book that's too difficult, they allow this free choice. The rationale is that if they insist a student read an appropriately leveled book, the student would feel that classmates notice the "easier" book and may mock the student. As a result, the student's self-confidence may suffer. But think about this—a child who chooses a book that's too hard spends the entire independent reading time "pretending" to read and thereby self-confirming that she or he is not as capable as others. As the student stares at the page full of words, what must be going on in the student's head? The student looks at friends and the teacher—they're all staring at the page as well, but they seem to be enjoying themselves. That doesn't help: it only adds to the mystery of "how to" read; it quietly and continually damages self-confidence.

But success does build confidence. So, in the model I'm suggesting, independent reading time gives students an opportunity to be truly involved with reading. Each student reads at a level of success (determined by the formative reading assessment), occasionally confers with a teacher about reading, and has the opportunity to share something with the class about reading. In short, independent reading gives a student an opportunity to get off the sidelines of reading and to get into the game. Jeffery Wilhelm describes this involvement as taking a student to "that place where a reader is totally absorbed in the experience of living through and conversing with the text" (hmmm… this sounds like flow). In my experience, and the experience of my colleagues, this involvement in reading occurs when the student is reading (really reading!) at a level that reflects the student's strengths as a reader. We've all seen the looks on students' faces when they feel the success of true involvement—it's wonderful!

Fielding and Pearson state that four components are necessary for students to be involved in instruction that maximizes the possibility of comprehension. These components are

- large amounts of time for actual text reading
- teacher-directed instruction in comprehension strategies
- opportunities for peer and collaborative learning
- occasions for students to talk to a teacher and one another about their responses to reading

Here's a workable classroom model of independent reading that allows students to become better readers *and* allows time for informal classroom assessment.

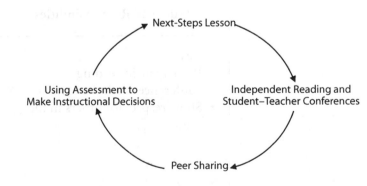

Establishing the Classroom Routine

1. Define the roles of the teacher and students during independent reading time.

While I'm a strong advocate for students reading appropriately leveled books, I'm not suggesting that students who struggle should read books that "look" like the books of beginning readers. Many publishers have responded to the need for lower-level books that are of interest to older readers. Contact the educational publishers and have a look at what's available—you may be pleasantly surprised.

It may take several weeks to get to the classroom routine in place, so don't rush it. Start with a few minutes of independent reading and slowly build up to 20 or 30 minutes.

2. Teach the students how to choose a book at a comfortable reading level.
3. Schedule time each day for independent reading.

Establishing the Classroom Routine

Students' Responsibilities	Teacher's Responsibilities
• Respect each other's abilities • Choose a book that is at a comfortable reading level (reading is accurate and fluent).	• Teach the class about respecting each other's abilities • Teach the class how to choose a book at a comfortable reading level (reading is accurate and fluent) • Schedule a daily time for independent reading

Student–Teacher Conferences

Once the students have the routine of reading well-chosen books in place, plan to begin your informal reading assessments. Each day, prepare to do a reading record, make your assessment notes about the student's reading, and have a conversation with the student about his or her reading. Initially, you'll have time for only one assessment each day, but as you become more comfortable with the procedure, you'll be able to check in with two or three students daily. But don't rush yourself. Take your time to be comfortable with the routine. This time should be as pleasant for you as it is for your students—since you're listening to the student read a passage with at least 90% accuracy and a good level of fluency, it should be a positive time. At first, you'll want to do a complete reading assessment on each student. Once this is complete, the Short-Form Reading Assessment (see page 70) may be a sufficient check for progress.

Student–Teacher Conferences

Students' Responsibilities	Teacher's Responsibilities
• Read • Participate in reading conferences with the teacher • Show respect for others in the class	• Complete a reading record or short-form "check-in" reading assessment • Give each student feedback about what he/she is doing well and, when appropriate, a suggestion about what to try next • Observe the student's use of reading strategies throughout the day

The Short-Form Reading Assessment (page 70) allows for two "check-in" conferences on one page. This allows the teacher to easily refer to the previous check in, note progress, and chat with the student about gains made or future directions.

Peer Sharing

To close each session, a few students have an opportunity to share something about their reading with classmates.

Peer Sharing

Students' Responsibilities	Teacher's Responsibilities
• Be prepared to discuss something learned, something noticed, something questioned, or something connected	• Provide an opportunity for students to share information about what they've read, or a strategy that worked well as they read

Using Assessment to Inform Instruction

At the end of the day, teachers review their notes and make note of trends: what are students doing well, what are the areas of focus for instruction (see chapter 8). With this information, and in consultation with curriculum standards, next-steps strategy lessons are planned. Depending on classroom trends, these lessons may be presented to small groups, in a guided reading format, or to the whole class.

Does this mean that all of our experiences have been positive and that everywhere we go students are successful? No, we all realize that this is the real world, and there are long roads ahead of us. But we've noticed an increase in the engagement with reading in all students, and the successes—sometimes with the most resistant students—make the journey worthwhile.

> This model reflects the ongoing classroom work carried out by the group of literacy coordinators with whom I work. Over the past few years, we've experienced some wonderful successes with students of all ages and abilities. Here are some examples of student quotes passed on to me by my colleagues Bev White, Isaac MacEachen, Pat Wadden, and Mike Coughlan.
>
> - "This is so great... I didn't know I was supposed to think while I was reading!"
> - "Reading rules!"
> - "Do you mean we're allowed to think about other things while we read?"
> - "Why didn't we know about this stuff before?"
> - "Are you coming to our class today? I love reading!".
> - "Hey, Reading Lady, got any good books?"
> - "I used to think poetry was stupid—now I can use it to let my mind grow around the words."
> - "It's really about making sense of it all, it's not about just getting the words right."
> - "Now that I don't have to read only what the teacher says, reading is okay!"

Short-Form Reading Assessment

Name:

Date: Title: Level:

Accuracy: Fluency:

Notes (sources of information used; evidence of noticing, searching, and checking; comprehension strategies used; general notes):

Accuracy: Fluency:

Notes (sources of information used; evidence of noticing, searching, and checking; comprehension strategies used; general notes)

The Next-Steps Lesson

Based on the trends noticed from the reading assessment, teachers make choices about appropriate next-steps lessons (see chapter 9 for more). The next-steps lessons are short and explicit, and they focus on what good readers do. These lessons are directed by the teacher and allow increasing opportunities for student involvement. Together, the teacher and the students think about how to process various types of text more effectively.

Topics covered during these lessons include

- respecting strengths
- how to choose a book for independent reading
- becoming aware of what we already do when we read
- how to access prior knowledge
- how to determine importance
- how to make connections
- how to synthesize information
- how to infer
- how to question
- how to word solve
- how to create sensory images
- how to predict

Although these lessons appear to separate the comprehension strategies into individual processes, the goal is to encourage students to see how all the strategies work together. In my classroom, I've presented these lessons in two ways. Depending on the situation, both are effective.

- These lessons can be presented as a brief mini lesson at the beginning of independent reading time. After the lessons, the students think about the strategy as they read independently.
- These lessons can be presented midway through independent reading time. This allows students to think about what they've just been reading and apply it to the lesson.

Since these lessons are short and very focused, teachers may want to elaborate on the lessons during time set aside for guided or shared reading.

The Next-Steps Lesson

Students' Responsibilities	Teacher's Responsibilities
• Participate in small- or large-group lesson	• Using trends noticed in the formative reading assessments, prepare lessons that build on existing strengths and provide direct instruction about the next step

Perhaps the most interesting observation about this model for independent reading time is that it causes some teachers to feel guilty—the students are so involved with their reading and they enjoy the conferences so much that, as one teacher said, "I know the kids are all enjoying themselves, but it just doesn't feel like they're working or that I'm working." My response? Don't worry—these are some of the most valuable moments of the day. We know that the more students read, the better readers they become. We also know that students choose to read when they are interested in the text and when they are *able to read the text*. This model of independent reading time simply allows students to become better readers. The student–teacher conferences require a teacher to use all his or her knowledge of the reading process to listen, observe, assess, and give feedback. (That's a lot of work!) And, as to not "not feeling like work?"—isn't that the definition of a flow experience?

Using Assessment Results to Make Instructional Choices

Planning Lessons

The first step in using the information we gather through informed assessment is organizing the information. The Planning Chart on page 75 allows the teacher to summarize the information gathered from the reading assessment.

Here's an example of a planning chart filled in. Notes on filling it in appear in regular type, and sample notes appear in italics.

Name:	Date:

Next Steps for Instruction:
Although this is the last section filled in, it's at the top for easy reference. Teacher reviews the information in the chart below and determines a focus for instruction.
Focus on effective word work—lesson on searching for known parts of words (chunking) and putting them together —then check for meaning and structure

Instructional Level – *H*	Sources of information Used	Evidence of Noticing, Searching and Checking	Comprehension Strategies Used
Text possibilities: Teacher lists possibilities of books to use for instruction	**Strengths:** Teacher lists what sources of information the student uses effectively. *Bill uses meaning and structure information well; his substitutions are meaningful.*	**Strengths:** Teacher lists the problem-solving strategies the student uses effectively. *Bill notices when things don't make sense and will reread a sentence to search for more information.*	**Strengths:** Teacher lists the comprehension strategies the student uses effectively *Bill creates sensory images well.*
	Thinking ahead: Teacher notes possibilities for instruction in using the sources of information. *Increase Bill's accuracy and automaticity with word-solving strategies.*	**Thinking Ahead:** Teachers notes possibilities for instruction to develop problem-solving strategies. *Add to Bill's searching strategies —as he rereads, think … what am I looking for?*	**Thinking Ahead:** Teacher notes possibilities for instruction to develop comprehension strategies. *Use sensory images to aid in making inferences.*

Our goal is to plan lessons that have a definite purpose, that engage the students, that the students see as useful, and that provide the right amount of challenge. Too much challenge, and the student becomes disengaged; too little challenge, and the student becomes disengaged. Just the right amount of challenge, and the student is more likely to become engaged with the lesson, and involved with the text, the task, and the learning.

Throughout this book, I've been talking about the merits of using assessment to identify student strengths and using the assessment results to plan instruction that builds on these strengths. Instruction that builds, or scaffolds, on existing abilities is much more likely to lead to situations where what we teach is learned by our students. Why? Because instruction that is built on strengths is delivered at what is known as an "optimal instructional level," and is most likely to lead that wonderful time in a learning experience when everything falls into place.

The optimal instructional level was clearly defined when Russian psychologist Lev Vygotsky (1896–1934) described the concept of the "zone of proximal development." Simply stated, the zone of proximal development describes the opportunity for instruction that exists between a student's actual knowledge and potential knowledge. This concept states that the student's actual knowledge, which is known through various forms of assessment, in combination with the influence of a teacher who teaches at a level that provides just enough challenge for a student, will become the student's potential knowledge. In other words, the teacher's lesson provides a scaffold between the actual knowledge and the potential knowledge. For the purposes of classroom instruction, teaching "within the zone" means the teacher is aware of student strengths and has a good grasp of what elements and concepts make up the curriculum standards. Learning "within the zone" means a student can use what he or she knows, along with just enough support and pressure from the teacher, to meet the challenges of the lesson.

The first step in planning a lesson at the optimal instructional level, or in the zone of proximal development is to stop, think, and question:

- What do I know about my students' abilities?
- What's the next logical step in their learning?
- Is it clear to me how this lesson bridges the known with the new?
- Which instructional-level text will be used?
- What will I look for as evidence of a teaching–learning match?

Initially, these questions require a lot of thought. But the more a teacher uses formative reading assessments, the more knowledge that teacher gains about the reading process and about planning next-steps lessons. In gathering information about reading and connecting the information to what we know, we are better able make sense of the entire process of reading.

The Repertoire of Literacy Practices

Nowadays, a teacher who wants a lesson on any subject can simply pick up a book, look up a certain topic, and—voilà—there's a ready-made lesson. Or, even faster, the teacher can do an internet search. But I'd like to offer a word of caution. It's easy to become seduced by the huge numbers of strategy activities and to forget about the importance of identifying the purpose of the lesson—to determine how it will increase each student's ability to process text effectively.

It's not just about asking the students to "do" the strategy activity, it's about creating a lesson that allows the student to see how to use the strategy. The pur-

Planning Chart

Name:		Date:	
Next Steps for Instruction:			
Instructional Level	**Sources of information Used**	**Evidence of Noticing, Searching, and Checking**	**Comprehension Strategies Used**
Text possibilities:	Strengths:	Strengths:	Strengths:
	Thinking Ahead:	Thinking Ahead:	Thinking Ahead:

pose of a strategy lesson is for the student to learn *how to* use the strategy, and then use it in a flexible way.

For example, if creating a visual image helps a student understand how a family in a novel about the pioneers faced hardships, he is using the strategy of creating a visual image. If he then applies his ability to use visual images to solve a math problem, he's using the strategy in a flexible way. And when the student becomes aware of the fact that it really is best to use several strategies in concert (e.g., connections between visual images allow inferences to be created), he'll be actively involved in effective processing of text.

To achieve this flexibility and to avoid teaching strategies as isolated activities, it's helpful to think of the goals of the next-steps lessons as falling under an umbrella that Luke and Freebody refer to as a "repertoire of practices." This repertoire of practices highlights the importance of actively thinking while reading. Actively thinking allows the reader to interact with the text and to make choices about how to interpret, question, and use the text. Learners become able to

- break the code of texts: recognizing and using the fundamental features and architecture of written texts including alphabet, sounds in words, spelling, conventions and patterns of sentence structure and text
- participate in the meaning of text: understanding and composing meaningful written, visual, and spoken texts from the meaning systems of particular cultures, institutions, families, communities, nation-states, and so forth
- use texts functionally: traversing the social relations around texts; knowing about and acting on the different cultural and social functions that various texts perform both inside and outside school, and knowing that these functions shape the way texts are structured, their tone, their degree of formality, and their sequence of components
- critically analyze and transform texts: understanding and acting on the knowledge that texts are not neutral; that they represent particular views and silence other points of view, and influence people's ideas; and that their designs and discourses can be critiqued and redesigned in novel ways. (Luke and Freebody)

I always try to match what I read in the research with what I learn from my students. So whenever I meet a group of students, I ask them to tell me what they think about reading. Without fail, their comments reflect the interrelatedness modeled by Luke and Freebody's repertoire of practices.

Grade 3 Students' Responses to "What Do You Think About Reading?"

- *Reading is understanding words and putting them into sentences, paragraphs, and stories.*
- *Reading is either getting information or using your imagination.*
- *Reading is like a movie to me because when I read I can picture the writing in my head and then I think of what the picture means.*
- *Reading lets you think about things in different ways.*
- *I read to find an answer and I end up asking even more questions.*

Grade 10 Students' responses to "What Do You Think About Reading?"

- *When I read, I go into the page.*
- *Sometimes, I'm confused, but I just keep reading and things fall into place.*

If a student says she can make pictures in her head, does that guarantee that she understands better? I'm not sure it does. It may be a start, but I think she has to know how to use those pictures to make connections, inferences, or predictions with the information in the text.

Repertoire is defined as a "range" or "collection"—both of these words suggest working together, rather than working in isolation. Although we may introduce a strategy in isolation, the purpose of the lesson is to allow the reader to build on the existing strategies that enable the reader to use the whole repertoire of practices more effectively.

- *Sometimes the big words are important, sometimes they're not—you have to know how to decide.*
- *Reading lets me change my mind about things.*
- *You have to know that sometimes what you read isn't true—you have to be able to decide what you think.*

On the other hand, when students don't use the full repertoire of practices, they may not experience as much success. Here are some examples from a Grade 8 class:

- *I read fine, I just don't understand what I read.*
- *I have to read something 100 times to get it.*
- *I can't read well; there are too many words to remember.*
- *When I see a tricky word, I just make something up and keep reading.*
- *As soon as I read something, I forget it.*
- *I just don't see the point of reading!*
- *I'd rather pick up a wrench than a book.*

The most powerful instruction allows students to see the connectedness of lessons and the interweaving of strategies. These are the strategies that turn the marks on the page into words, and the words on the page into thoughts, and the thoughts on the page into meaningful and useful concepts. So as you think about the student's next-steps lessons, think about the purpose of the lesson and how this purpose allows the student to build on his repertoire of practices.

Since our goal is to teach students how to process text effectively, teaching the next-steps lesson is often best accomplished when the purpose for the lesson is clearly understood by the students. We want our students to know why we've chosen this lesson, how to complete the accompanying activity, how it will be useful, and how it will lead them to more questions and more learning.

9

Next-Steps Lessons

The lessons suggested in this chapter will help a teacher set up independent reading time as the time to carry out formative reading assessments. They have been developed by teachers throughout the world and have been adapted by my colleagues and me. No two teachers will present these lessons in exactly the same way—it's important that teachers feel comfortable customizing the lessons to fit their teaching style and to meet the abilities of each student, each small group of students, or each class of students. These lessons work as well for whole group instruction as they do in a small-group setting. They can (and should) be adapted to any level and any subject area. While the first four lessons target the younger grades, they can be adapted for older students. It's important that students understand that the strategies they use to process text in language arts are the same strategies that can be applied to reading a science or math text. It's also important for students to know that the same reading strategies, with varying levels of text, are used in the first year of school, in the last year of school, and after a person finishes school.

Here are a few notes to assist preparation:

- Teachers need more reading material and a wider range of reading material in their classrooms. Additional books, magazines, vertical files of fiction and nonfiction text, and websites provide an alternate view or a different wording of the information contained in the official text of the course. This sounds expensive, but doesn't have to be. An appeal to parents to send in current magazine or newspaper articles usually yields great results. Keeping these in file folders greatly increases the length of their life and utility. It's also a great idea for students to celebrate their birthdays by presenting a book to the class.
- Time to read should be a regular part of each school day—and it doesn't have to be confined to language arts time. In junior high and high school, students benefit from reading passages that relate to the subject by a variety of authors, from variety of points of view, at a variety of levels.
- Each lesson should be presented in a way that allows for maximum participation by the students.

My wish for schools? To increase the range and variety of fiction and nonfiction text in every classroom. A wide range of reading choices is crucial if every teacher's goal is to teach students become better readers.

Steps for Instruction

Although this list is presented as a series of discrete steps, I'm not suggesting such a regimented approach be used. This list simply allows the teacher to keep a mental note of the components of a lesson.

To teach a next-steps strategy lesson, include these elements:

1. Tell the students the topic or strategy that will be taught and why you've decided to teach it.
2. Using a demonstration, provide explicit instruction in the strategy.
3. Ask students to participate in the demonstration and observe their responses carefully. Clarify any confusion.
4. Assign independent practice of the strategy.
5. As students work independently, observe their work and give them feedback.
6. Use these observations to inform future instructional decisions.

Setting the Stage for Independent Reading

Lesson 1: Respecting Strengths

1. Tell the students the topic or strategy that will be taught and why you've decided to teach it.

Teacher: Today, we're going to learn about respecting each other's strengths in reading. Everyone is different and everyone has different abilities. It's important that we know what we can do well and that we see our classmates for what they are able to do.

2. Using a demonstration, provide explicit instruction.

Teacher: Some of you are very good at _____ (list a variety of abilities related to reading, writing, speaking, listening, visualizing, connecting, etc.) For example, I've noticed that _____ _____ (teacher mentions a few students and what they do well: *Jim is really good at listening to stories*).

3. Ask students to participate in the demonstration.

Teacher: I'd like you to tell me about what you're good at in reading.

At this point, students offer suggestions about whether they like listening to stories, creating pictures in their heads, guessing what will happen next, etc. The teacher charts these responses, observes carefully, and interjects with comments about abilities she or he has noticed about students. At the end of the discussion, each child should have a strength written by his or her name; see chart below. Teachers need to prepare well for this discussion, and should have notes gathered about students' levels of participation in class discussions about books, writing activities, reading activities, etc.

Name	Is a Good Reader Because
Jill	I draw good pictures about the story.
Fred	I listen to stories well.
Jamal	I tell other people about the stories I hear.
Sarah	I use lots of expression when I read
Tamarah	I know what books my friends might like to read.
Bob	I like to pretend I'm a character in the story.
Jose	I read my own stories to my sister.
Malcolm	I have a good imagination

4. Assign independent practice.

Place the Being a Good Reader form (page 81) on an overhead projector and demonstrate how to fill it out. Then cut a paper copy of the form into strips. Each student gets one strip of each statement. Class results can be charted, compared, and referred to in future lessons. Younger students like to attach these strips to their name or to a picture of themselves.

5. As students work independently, observe their work and give them feedback.

6. Use these observations to inform future instructional decisions.

Lesson 2: Teaching Students How to Listen

Debbie Miller describes how well her students participate in discussions about good listening skills. They seem to have all the answers about what it means to be a good listener. The problem is, after the discussion these students often return to their old ways of interrupting, groaning at comments, and responding without consideration of a person's feelings. Her frustration is clear:

> But their behavior didn't change. And I'd wonder, "What's wrong here?" "Why don't they get it" And even sometimes, "What's wrong with these kids, anyway?" Eventually, I realized, of course that nothing was wrong with "these kids." They didn't get it because I hadn't *shown them how*. I'd *told* them to be respectful, thoughtful, and kind, but I hadn't shown them what that looks and sounds like. (Miller, p. 18)

Being a Good Reader

I Like…; I Don't Like…; I Want to Be Better at…

I Like _____because

I Like _____because

I Like _____because

I Like _____because

I don't like _____because

I don't like _____because

I don't like _____because

I want to be better at _____because

I want to be better at _____because

I want to be better at _____because

I want to be better at _____because

Miller's final words, "what listening looks like *and* sounds like" are crucial. Listening, for children and adults, is more than sitting up straight and making eye contact. Actually, this listening posture can quite effectively mask an inability to, or a choice not to, listen. As teachers, our authentic demonstration of what listening looks like and sounds like, and authentic lessons about how to listen effectively, are important.

1. *Tell the students the topic or strategy that will be taught and why you've decided to teach it.*

   Teacher: Today, we're going to learn about how to listen. Listening is very important. When we listen, we send a message that we care about what the other person is saying. And when we listen well, we help ourselves to understand. Listening to someone means you're showing them respect.

2. *Using a demonstration, provide explicit instruction.*

At first, the demonstrations about listening can be somewhat dramatic—you want to make a point. Before the school day begins, ask a student to participate in a role play with you. Once class begins, ask the student to tell you about something that happened at recess. As the student tells the story, exaggerate your poor listening skills— fiddle with something, interrupt, start telling your own story, etc.

3. *Ask students to participate in the demonstration.*

Ask the students to talk about your listening skills and how you made the speaker feel. Chart the responses and discuss.

4. *Assign independent practice.*

This independent practice should be authentic. Tell the students that you are going to watch for "good listeners" everyday.

5. *As students work independently, observe their work and give them feedback.*

Over the next few days, keep an eye out (an ear out?) for students who are listening effectively in class, in the playground, in the hall, etc. When you see someone listening well, point it out to the individual. And make sure you practise your own good listening skills.

6. *Use these observations to inform future instructional decisions.*

Once the students have a sense of how independent reading requires each of them to respect their classmates' strengths and to show respect by using their listening skills, teachers can begin lessons that allow students to make effective book choices.

Lesson 3: Choosing a Book for Independent Reading

Time frame: Several lessons

1. **Tell the students the topic or strategy that will be taught and why you've decided to teach it.**

   Teacher: We're going to start learning about how to choose books that are just right for independent reading. We're going to learn about choosing a book we're interested in, the five-finger rule, and why reading fluently is important. Independent reading time is a time to practise what we do well. We choose books that allow us to relax and think about the story and not spend too much time working out tricky words.

2. **Using a demonstration, provide explicit instruction.**

   The teacher reads a story to the class and makes quite a few errors. She or he asks what the students think of the reading and if they think the teacher understands it.

3. **Ask students to participate in the demonstration.**

   Teacher: How do you decide if a book is not too hard for you?

   Teacher divides student responses into categories. (See example in box below.)

4. **Assign independent practice.**

   During independent reading time, it becomes the student's responsibility to choose a book she or he can read accurately and fluently.

5. **As students work independently, observe their work and give them feedback.**

   Notice how the level of text affects the student's involvement with various lessons.

6. **Use these observations to inform future instructional decisions.**

> **Teacher:** How do you know when a book is just right for you?
>
> As the students respond, the teacher makes notes on a chart paper. After a few minutes, the teacher suggests that they look at a list created from their responses.
>
> **Teacher:** You've come up with a lot of ways to describe a book that's just right for you. I think we can put these ideas into categories. Here are some categories we can try.
>
> She shows them a chart, and they decide together which comments go under each heading. Their results look like this:

Choosing a Comfortable Book to Read

Not Too Hard	I Can Read it Like a Storyteller	I'm Interested in the Topic
It's not too hard. I don't make a lot of mistakes. When I read it, I don't make a lot of mistakes. I can tell someone else what it's about.	I can read it to my book buddy. I can read it to my mom. I can read some to my friend, so they'll read it too.	It's interesting. The cover is interesting. There are good pictures. I can read some to my friend, so they'll read it too.

Involving the students in this lesson allows them to feel they are involved in the deciding what a "comfortable book" actually is. They agree that they'll use these categories when describing or choosing a book that they feel very comfortable reading.

The topic headings of "Not Too Hard" and "I Can Read it Like a Storyteller" and "I'm Interested in the Topic" are the crux of effective book choice. So, for the next few days, using the lesson format suggested above, she teaches them the about accuracy and the importance of reading fluently.

Lesson 4: The Five-Finger Rule

This lesson defines what students mean by "too hard." The five-finger rule is loosely based on the idea that a student's independent reading level is based on an accuracy rate of 95%. Simply stated, the five-finger rule is this:

As you read, put a finger on the table each time you meet a tricky word. A tricky word is a word you don't understand or a word you can't decode. If, before you read 100 words, you put five fingers on the table, the book is too hard.

After teaching this lesson, the teacher puts on the table a variety of books that will allow all students to find at least one or two that reflect their comfortable reading level. Then students practise using the five-finger rule and find the book(s) that suit them best.

Once comfortable with this method of book choice, it's time to move on. Remember that with each lesson, we're building on what the students are able to do. The next focus of these lessons on effective book choice is to teach students the importance of reading fluently.

Lesson 5: The Importance of Reading Fluently

Here's a lesson that I've used, with a slight variation of text and/or genre, with several different grade levels.

Choose a poem the class will enjoy. Before presenting it to the class, practise reading it in a nonfluent way. Change the phrasing, change the intonation, ignore some of the punctuation marks, and don't stop at the end of lines. Then, without showing the students the text, read the poem in this nonfluent way. Ask for their reactions.

Here's an example I've used with older students and teachers. I read this with little intonation. The slashes indicate where I made pauses in the first reading. (I didn't pause at the ends of lines.)

Freedom, California
By Spencer Critchley

A / young man by / the highway
Is spittin' / at / the moon
Wavin' / and jumpin' up / and down
Until / the exhaustion
Makes/ him change / his tune
Now he / is down flat out on / the ground

You might / hear him shouting
As / you pass him by
"I've / had about / enough of Minnesota"
He's / writing / the words
With / his finger on / the sky
"My / new home is / Freedom, California"

[You can probably stop here… the class will probably be getting restless]

You think of the distance
Put her in reverse
Find him there ready with his pack
He digs out a bible
Things are looking worse
Turns out it's a diary in the back

He says welcome to my story
As I make my getaway
I've had about enough of Minnesota
It's easy to move on
When you got no place to stay
My new home is Freedom, California

A young man in the desert
Heading on his way
Dust looks like he's walking on the air
He's holding a twenty
You signed it with your name
Told him not to spend it till he's there

You might hear him laughing
As he fades away
"You're never gonna find me Minnesota!"
He's off on the wind
He's what the wind would say
And his new home is Freedom, California

Here's a typical reaction to my reading:

Me: So, what did you think of the poem?
Class: (Blank stares all around.)
Me: What was it about?
Class: (Shrugged shoulders) We don't know.
  Something about a highway or a moon, and some spitting.
Me: Could you picture the characters in the story?
Class: No.
Me: Why don't you know what the characters were like?
Class: We didn't understand it.
Me: Why didn't you understand it? Were the words hard?
Class: No, the words were easy, but the way you read it made it hard to understand.
Me: How did I read it?
Class: All choppy.
Me: Choppy? What do you mean by choppy? Can you show me with your hand what choppy reading looks like?
Class: (Move their hands in an abrupt, repetitive up-and-down motion.)
Me: Hmmmm, may I try to read it to you again?
Class: Yes. (But the class is usually hesitant—after the first experience, they don't ever seem to want me to read again!)
Me: (After reading to the class again, this time fluently, with phrasing, intonation, and expression) How was that?
Class: Better!
Me: Can you tell me what it was about?
Class: (They proceed to tell me their interpretation of the words to the poem.)
Me: Can you picture the young man?
Class: (Provides descriptions)
Me: Does this remind you of anything?
Class: (Provides all sorts of connections)
  It's like the times of the hippies, everyone was hitchhiking then.
  Actually, I think this is a song—it's like a country and western type of song.
  This reminded me of a lot of things, but what I really want to talk about is why the guy signed his name on the money.
Me: Why can you understand so much better this time?
Class: The way you read it let us understand.
Me: You said my first reading was choppy. How would you describe this reading?
Class: Like this. (They move their hands in a wavy motion.)

Students learn from these lessons that, during independent reading time, it's their responsibility to choose a book that they are interested in and can read accurately and fluently, and to respect the choices of the other students. With this established, teachers can begin to circulate among the students and gather information about their reading. At first, teachers should complete a reading record on each student. Then, a check-in assessment is all that may be needed (see page 70).

Comprehension Strategies

Once independent reading time is established, the next-steps lessons focus on demonstrating a comprehension strategy. Comprehension strategies include

- Accessing prior knowledge
- Creating sensory images
- Connecting
- Questioning
- Predicting
- Determining importance
- Fix-up strategies
- Synthesizing
- Inferring

As I mentioned earlier, there are many excellent books and internet sites that provide suggestions for instruction in comprehension strategies, so I'll not attempt to replicate what's already been done. I will, however, provide one example of how to set up these lessons so the purpose is clear, the lessons build on strengths, and the students see a usefulness of the strategy.

Lesson 6: Acknowledging What We Do; Thinking about What We Could Do

1. *Tell the students the topic or strategy that will be taught and why you've decided to teach it.*

   Teacher: Today, we're going to stop and think about our reading. There's lots more to reading than just knowing what the story (or topic) is about. As we read, we should take the time to stop and think about what's going on in our heads as we read.

2. *Using a demonstration, provide explicit instruction.*

3. *Ask students to participate in the demonstration.*

The teacher reads a short passage to the class. Depending on the subject, this can be a piece of fiction or nonfiction of any genre. While reading, the teacher pauses every once in awhile to talk about what the passage makes the teacher think of. The teacher shares his or her thoughts with the class, and then asks for students' response to the text.

4. *Assign independent practice.*

Students begin reading the books chosen for independent reading.

5. *As students work independently, observe their work and give them feedback.*

After 10 to 15 minutes, the teacher asks them to discuss, or use a sticky note to record, what their story made them think of. The teacher collects these comments. Later in the day, the teacher goes through these notes and decides which of the comprehension strategies the students are already using.

6. *Use these observations to inform future instructional decisions.*

The next day, the teacher shares this information and commends the class on what they are already doing. The teacher also mentions that they'll be learning about how each of these strategies help them to become better readers.

Teacher: All of the comments you made are great indicators of the type of thinking that goes on in our heads as we read. I've put your comment on sticky notes and I'm going to show you what great thinkers you already are.

[One by one, the teacher attaches the sticky notes to one of the rays coming out of a diagram of a head. As she attaches the sticky note, she explains what each ray means.]

- *Accessing prior knowledge* means you thought about what you already know.
- *Visualizing* means creating a picture, or some other sensory image, in your head.
- *Connecting* means the text reminded you of something that happened to you, something you read or saw, or something that is occurring in the world.
- *Questioning* means something puzzled you and you knew you had to look for an answer.
- *Predicting* means you used the information you had to make a logical guess about what will happen next.
- *Determining importance* means you were aware of what information was essential to the text and what information provided a support.
- *Fix-up strategies* means you were aware that something didn't seem right, and it was your responsibility to solve the problem.
- *Synthesizing* means you put pieces of information together so they fit—like a puzzle.
- *Inferring* means you used some information from the story to make an assumption about the story, the character, or the event.

While completing this activity, some students ask if a sticky note could go in more than one place—it seemed as if more than one strategy was being used. The answer to this question is a definite yes, as no one strategy works in isolation. Another student commented that the way she felt about the story also affected her use of strategies—since she enjoyed reading it, and was comfortable reading it, she used all sorts of these strategies. But, she said, she may not have used so many if she hadn't enjoyed it. Absolutely! Our affective domain has a huge impact on our cognitive domain.

The next step of this lesson includes a bit of assessment that the class can be involved in. After the students have put the sticky notes on the diagram, look for trends. Are some strategies used more frequently than others? Usually visualizing and connecting top the list. This gives you and the class some information. If the class is using certain strategies a lot, that's an indication of what they are able to do. So if your class or group of students demonstrate a lot of visualizing, your next lesson may be to teach how visualizing works in a different type of text, perhaps nonfiction. Looking for trends also gives the teacher an idea of what strategies are most often taught… teachers often teach in a way that reflects their own learning style. Being aware of a wider range of strategies encourages a teacher to think of alternate ways to present information.

> *This lesson works well with all ages and all types of text. I've even used it as a non-text experience. I gave every student an object (I used beach glass) and asked them to use a sticky note to write everything, literal and figurative, that came to their mind. Then they decided on which comprehension strategy the sticky note should be placed. When finished, all the strategies listed above were used. The power of using an object instead of a piece of text is in how it demonstrates that the strategies often associated with comprehending text are actually strategies associated with all learning.*

Once these introductory lessons are in place, teachers and students can open up the possibilities for exploring all sorts of text. There are lots of good professional books full of great ideas for strategy lessons. As I mentioned earlier, it's important to think beyond the strategy activity and decide what the purpose of the lesson is for this group of students at this time. Your goal is to teach the students how to do the strategy and then how to use it in a flexible way.

This lesson gives you information about class *trends—individual use of comprehension strategies can be assessed by using the comprehension assessment on pages 46–54.*

Once you've decided on a focus for your instruction, a quick comprehension strategy lesson at the beginning of independent reading time allows students to focus their thinking on a particular strategy. At the end of independent reading time, students can share how they used this strategy (or other strategies) as they read. The goal is for students to stop, think, and become aware of what goes on in their heads as they read, and how this allows them to understand the text better.

The following suggestions allow teachers to collect more evidence about the students' use of comprehension strategies.

Lesson 7: Collecting Evidence About Strategy Use

Reflecting on a Strategy

This reflection may be completed together orally, on sticky notes, or as a written assignment in the student's notebook. Use the Reflecting on a Strategy form on page 91 as a framework for a discussion or written response.

During independent reading time, students should be encouraged to explore a variety of genres—it's not just about reading novels or stories.

> *Here's an example of a reflection I did with my class. As they made suggestions, I wrote their comments. I posted the results on the class bulletin board.*
>
> Our reflection about: making connections.
> Describe this comprehension strategy in your own words.
>
> - *It's like joining thoughts.*
> - *It's when two things can be paired.*
> - *It's when one thing let's you think about another.*
> - *If I read this, then I think of that.*
> - *If I can see what something's related to, I can understand it better.*
> - *It's not just one thing connected to one other; connections are like links in a chain...*
> - *Connections can lead you in lots of different directions.*

How will this comprehension strategy be useful?
- *It makes me remember to think of a story like a story board.*
- *I'll think about all the connections between different events, and I'll remember a story better.*
- *I'll use it when we do a time line.*
- *I'll think about how all the things that I study for a test are connected to what the test is about.*

Double Entry Diary

Another way for students to reflect on reading is to use a double entry diary. The simplicity of a double entry diary is what makes it so useful.

After a strategy lesson, students spend some time reading their independent-reading book. As they read, their task is to find a powerful phrase or sentence that causes them to stop and think about how they used the strategy in the opening lesson. On the double entry diary, students write down the quote or powerful words, and their response. Use the Double Entry Diary form on page 92.

The size of this double entry diary is important. The goal is for the student to make a quick note of his or her use of a strategy, so the small size is perfect. When the space is small, some students tend to be more willing to write.

For a more focused response, try a composite diary format. After students have been taught the various strategies, they should be on the lookout for powerful phrases or sentences that encourage them to stop, think, and better understand the text. The graphic organizer on pages 93–94 allows students to keep a running diary of their thoughts. There is no particular order in which the sections should be filled out; some sections may be used more than others; the form can be used as complete pages or separate sections.

My colleague Paul Healy gives his students a plastic sleeve (designed to hold trading cards) to keep the sections of the Composite Diary in. When students are finished reading a book, they have a a a diary of how they responded to the text.

Over time, and with lots of practice on well-chosen text, each strategy becomes a part of a student's repertoire of problem-solving skills. As the student gains control of a strategy, that student has the ability to choose to use it to problem solve in a variety of settings. Once the strategy becomes automatic, a student can access the same strategy for use in all subjects. These strategies will benefit all students. The opportunity to think beyond the page and to validate all that's going on in their minds is important. Students who struggle with reading begin to feel a sense of control when reading and realize that they have a way, or several ways, to work through the tricky sections of texts.

"Some students with learning disabilities think that they will fail before they even attempt a task. If they do perform well, many times these students will attribute it to luck or level of difficulty of the task (e.g., too easy). If they do poorly they will attribute it to their own lack of ability or effort. Students with learning disabilities need to be taught they are in control." (Wood and Dickinson)

As each comprehension strategy is taught, the journey begins again. Through the classroom focus on more time reading at a comfortable level, students will have more opportunities to use the strategy in a variety of ways and to experience success with their daily experiences with text. As students approach new learning, they can use a wider range of strategies to become more fully involved in the learning process. And since formative assessment is built into the process, the groundwork has been laid for teachers to plan lessons with an awareness of what students are able to do. Through this involvement, which is so heavily based on prospects of success, students are much more likely to experience a state of flow in their learning.

Reflecting on a Strategy

Our reflection about _____
                    (name of strategy)

Describe this comprehension strategy in your own words.

How will this comprehension strategy be used?

Double Entry Diary

Quote: Page:

Response:

Quote: Page:

Response:

Quote: Page:

Response:

Composite Diary

Making Connections	Making Inferences
Page: Date:	Page: Date:
Quote or Event:	Quote or Event:
This reminds me of	This makes me infer
This is useful because	This is useful because

Making Predictions	Questioning
Page: Date:	Page: Date:
Quote or Event:	Quote or Event:
This will lead to	This makes me wonder about
This is useful because	This is useful because

Composite Diary—*continued*

Creating Sensory Images	Fix-Up Strategies
Page: Date:	Page: Date:
Quote or Event:	Quote or Event:
This allows me to create an image of	I figured it out by
This is useful because	This is useful because
Synthesizing	**Determining Importance**
Page: Date:	Page: Date:
Quote or Event:	Quote or Event:
This was caused by	This is important because
This is useful because	This is useful because

Conclusion

Throughout this book, I've referred to Csikzsentmihalyi's notion of achieving a state of flow in the classroom. A state of flow is experienced when, as we often say, "everything we do just clicks." Flow experiences occur when we become completely involved in a task, knowing that the challenge is just right and the feedback we get will both allow us and encourage us to seek further challenges.

Based on my own teaching experiences, which span school entry to graduate-level courses, it's increasingly clear to me that achieving flow begins with using what we know. Discovering what we know about our students and what students know about themselves is the goal of assessment. Informal assessment allows the teacher to identify what a student is able to do and to plan instruction that builds on those abilities. The rationale for assessment is simple but powerful. It's about achievement—how achievement looks, where achievement leads us, and, most importantly for the student, how achievement feels. How does it feel? It feels like flow.

What do students think about all of this? Is flow something they acknowledge? Perhaps they don't call it flow, but they certainly have a sense of what flow feels like. Here are some thoughts, from students of all ages, who have been involved in the classroom model for formative reading assessment discussed in this book. Each student was asked *What do you think about reading?*

- *Reading is good for your brain and I think it is fun.*
- *Reading takes you right into the book and the characters are talking to you.*
- *Reading is cool—it's like a movie to me because when I read I can picture the writing, the characters, the setting, and the events in my head.*
- *Reading is when you read a book and find things out. I get in good with a book.*
- *Reading is organizing the words on the page in your head as thoughts and then everything makes sense.*
- *Reading is understanding the words and knowing that you can enjoy reflecting on them.*
- *Reading is when you take a book and sit on a chair or stand on the floor and just have fun reading.*
- *Thank heavens I can read—I don't know what I would do if I couldn't!*
- *Reading is not like a job; it's like a hobby.*

Yes… they know about flow.

Bibliography

Allington, R. (2001) *What Really Matters for Struggling Readers: Designing Research Based Programs.* New York, NY: Addison-Wesley Educational Publishers Inc.

Black, P. and William, D. "Inside the Black Box: Raising Standards Through Classroom Assessment." *Phi Delta Kappan*, October 1998.

Clay, M. (1991) *Becoming Literate: The Construction of Inner Control.* Portsmouth, NH: Heinemann.

Clay, M. (1993) *Reading Recovery: A Guidebook for Teacher in Training.* Portsmouth, NH: Heinemann.

Clay, Marie. (2002) *An Observation of Early Literacy Achievement.* Portsmouth, NH: Heinemann.

Costa, A.L. and Kallick, B. "Describing 16 Habits of Mind." http://www.habits-of-mind.net/

Critchley, D. (1992) *How Many Times Must A Man Turn His Head.* Bermuda: Island Press.

Critchley, D. (1994) *Shackles of the Past.* Bermuda: Island Press.

Csikzsentmihalyi, M. (1997) *Finding Flow.* New York, NY: Basic Books.

Fielding, L.G. and Pearson, D. "Synthesis of Research / Reading Comprehension: What Works" in *Ed. Leadership* , Feb. 1994, v. 51 n. 5; p. 62.

Fountas, I.C. and Pinnell, G.S. (1996) *Guided Reading: Good First Teaching for All Children.* Portsmouth, NH: Heinemann.

Fountas, I.C. and Pinnell, G.S. (2001) *Guiding Readers and Writers, Grades 3–6: Teaching Comprehension, Genre and Content Literacy.* Portsmouth, NH: Heinemann.

Fountas, I.C. and Pinnell, G.S. (1999) *Matching Books to Readers.* Portsmouth, NH: Heinemann.

Gardner, H., Csikzsentmihalyi, M., and Damon, W. (2001) *Good Work.* New York, NY: Basic Books.

Goodman, K.S. "Analysis of Oral Reading Miscues: applied psycholinguistics" in *Reading Research Quarterly*, 1969, 5; pp. 9–30.

Goodman, Y.M. and Burke, C.L. (1972) *Reading Miscue Inventory: Manual and Procedures for Diagnosis and Evaluation.* NY: Macmillan.

Harvey, S. and Goudvis, A. (2000) *Strategies That Work: Teaching Comprehension to Enhance Understanding.* Portland, ME: Stenhouse.

Keene, E.O. and Zimmermann, S. (1997) *Mosaic of Thought: Teaching Comprehension in a Reader's Workshop.* Portsmouth, NH: Heinemann.

LeHane, D. (2001) *Mystic River.* New York, NY: Harper Collins.

Luke, A. and Freebody, P. "A Map of Possible Practices: Further Notes on the Four Resources Model" in *Practically Primary*, 1999, Volume 4, No. 2.

McLaughlin, G. "SMOG grading: A new readability formula" in *Journal of Reading*, 1969, 12 (8); pp. 639–646.

Miller, D. (2002) *Reading With Meaning: Teaching Comprehension in the Primary Grades.* Portland, ME: Stenhouse.

Otto, W. "Forward" to Wilhelm, J.D. (2001) *Improving Comprehension With Think-Aloud Strategies.* New York, NY: Scholastic.

Reading 44: A Core Reading Framework. (1999) Program Services, North Vancouver School District 44.

Robb, L. (2000) *Teaching Reading in Middle School.* New York, NY: Scholastic.

Rog, L.J. (2003) *Guided Reading Basics.* Markham, ON: Pembroke.

Rose, D.H. and Meyer, A. (2002) *Teaching Every Student in the Digital Age: Universal Design for Learning.* Alexandria, VA: ASCD.

Sparks, D. "Assessment Without Victims: An Interview With Richard Stiggins" in *Journal of Staff Development,* Spring 1999, Vol. 20, No. 2.

Tankersley, K. (2003) *The Threads of Reading: Strategies for Literacy Development.* Alexandria, VA: ASCD.

Walker, C. and Schmidt, E. (2004) *Smart Tests.* Markham, ON: Pembroke.

Wilhelm, J. (2001) *Improving Comprehension With Think-Aloud Strategies.* New York, NY: Scholastic Inc.

Wood, K.D. and Dickinson, T.S. (2000) *Promoting Literacy in Grades 4–9: A Handbook for Teachers and Administrators.* New York, NY: Allyn & Bacon.

Index